Moodle 2.0 Multimedia Cookbook

Add images, videos, music, and much more to make your
Moodle course interactive and fun

Silvina P. Hillar

[PACKT] open source *
PUBLISHING   community experience distilled

BIRMINGHAM - MUMBAI

Moodle 2.0 Multimedia Cookbook

First published: May 2011

Production Reference: 1160511

Published by Packt Publishing Ltd.
32 Lincoln Road
Olton
Birmingham, B27 6PA, UK.

ISBN 978-1-849514-70-5

www.packtpub.com

Cover Image by Ed Maclean (edmaclean@gmail.com)

Credits

Author

Silvina P. Hillar

Reviewers

Dr. Nellie Deutsch

Louise Adele Jakobsen

Alex Little

Acquisition Editor

Sarah Cullington

Development Editor

Alina Lewis

Technical Editor

Sakina Kaydawala

Copy Editor

Leonard D'Silva

Project Coordinator

Jovita Pinto

Proofreader

Jonathan Todd

Indexer

Hemangini Bari

Production Coordinator

Aparna Bhagat

Cover Work

Aparna Bhagat

About the Author

Silvina P. Hillar has been teaching English since 1993. She has always had a great interest in teaching, writing, and composing techniques, and has done a lot of research on this subject.

She is an English Teacher, a Certified Legal Translator (English/Spanish), and has a Post Degree in Education (graduated with Honors).

She has been working in several schools and institutes with native English-speaking students and as an independent consultant for many international companies as an interpreter, translator, and e-learning activities developer.

She has always had a passion for technological devices concerning education. Earlier on, videos and cassettes were a must in her teaching lessons; computers were and still are present. Her brother Gastón C. Hillar designed some programs and games for her teaching. Lately, she is teaching using Moodle and Web 2.0. She believes that one of the most amazing challenges in education is bridging the gap between classic education and modern technologies.

She has been doing a lot of research on multimedia assets that enhance teaching and learning through VLE platforms. She tries to embed the learning of students through new resources that are appealing and innovative for them. Thus, multimedia stimulates different thinking skills as well as multiple intelligences. Silvina has also worked on *Moodle 1.9 English Teacher's Cookbook, Packt Publishing*.

She lives with her six year-old son, Nico. When not tinkering with computers, she enjoys traveling to the seaside with her son, with whom she spends most of the time at the beach.

You can reach her at silvinahillar@hotmail.com.

You can follow her on Twitter: http://twitter.com/silvinahillar.

Acknowledgement

I would like to thank the entire team at Packt Publishing Ltd, who have worked with me as an incredibly helpful team. Sarah Cullington, who trusted me to develop this idea into a book. She was always ready to help and gave good advice when I was in doubt. Sneha Harkut and Jovita Pinto, who guided me with time management and patience. Alina Lewis also guided me in the developing stage of the book and added very wise comments to my original writings. It was a pleasure to share a second writing process with her.

I would also like to thank Sakina Kaydawala, who has performed a great job as a Technical Editor. Many thanks to all my students, either real or virtual, who make it possible for me to be their teacher.

I wish to acknowledge my three reviewers: Dr. Nellie Deutsch, Louise Jakobsen, and Alex Little. They had been very kind and helpful with their comments and gave me good tips that I added to the different chapters. Thanks! I must also thank my proofreader Jonathan Todd for his thorough reviews.

I owe tremendous thanks to my wonderful six year-old son–Nico, who despite his age, was very patient and supportive in the writing process of the book. Besides, he was occasionally forced to play alone while I concentrated on my writing.

My parents Susana and Jose (my dad is also a writer), who always stand by me and support my decisions. My brother, Gastón C. Hillar, who helps me whenever I need him, as usual. My little two year-old nephew Kevin and my sister-in-law Vanesa S. Olsen with whom I spend time working and exploring Moodle, Web 2.0 resources among other VLE platforms.

About the Reviewers

Dr. Nellie Deutsch is a Canadian educator, who earned her doctorate from the University of Phoenix from the School of Advanced Studies. Her dissertation research focused on instructor experiences with technology in blended learning contexts in higher education around the world. Dr. Deutsch is the founder of Integrating Technology for Active Lifelong Learning (IT4ALL), a non-profit organization that provides professional development workshops for groups around the world on Moodle, e-portfolios, reflective practice, WebQuests, TESOL, ESOL, academic writing, Mahara, and other Web 2.0 tools for educators, generally in conjunction with different projects and initiatives. Dr. Deutsch is also the founder and current coordinator of the annual Connecting Online for Instruction and Learning, hosted online by http://it4all.org/ and supported by WiZiQ online learning platform. Dr. Deutsch has provided consultation on how to integrate Moodle and Elluminate learning environments for distance education at the Open University of Israel and worked as a consultant at http://wikieducator.org, supported by the Commonwealth of Learning (COL), Otago Polytechnic (New Zealand), and Athabasca Open University (Canada) in developing online courses and facilitation. She is also an educational consultant, mentor, instructional course designer, and online facilitator on how to integrate technology into the face-to-face and online classroom using Moodle, WebQuests, Professional Electronic Portfolios (PEP), Web 2.0 tools, social networks, and wikis. In addition, she is an accredited PAIRS (Practical Application of Intimate Relationship Skills) practitioner, conflict resolution practitioner, curriculum and instructional course designer and consultant, and mentor to educators around the world.

She has written two chapters in *Adventures in Collaborative Authoring: Education for a Digital World 2.0* by *Crown Publications, Victoria, BC. Canada*. She has also written a chapter on a book that is forthcoming from *Sage: Cases in Online Interview Research,* edited by *Janet Salmons,* to be published in the fall of 2011.

Louise Adele Jakobsen is passionate about the potential a wide range of technologies have to enhance learning and support teaching, business, and life. Recent roles and responsibilities that have enhanced her knowledge, understanding, and application of a variety of tools include being the eLearning Curriculum Manager at a large Further Education (FE) College in the UK with responsibility for moving forward the eLearning agenda; supporting and encouraging staff to use Moodle in more interactive and engaging ways; and Learning and Development Manager at a private training organization where Moodle was used to support organizational and work-based development. Her enthusiasm is evident through the various training, sharing, and motivating strategies that are used. She has experience of working in FE, Higher Education, Adult and Community Learning, and Local Government delivering high class training to teachers, managers, care staff, and small and medium businesses. Louise has also developed resources and delivered training for and on behalf of national organizations including NIACE and THinK FE. She completed her MSc in Multimedia and eLearning with the University of Huddersfield (UK) in 2008. Her interests / experiences include: Teaching and Learning, Technology, eLearning Pedagogies, Effective use of VLEs (especially Moodle), Designing eLearning resources, Using Social Networking tools in Education, Staff Development / training, and Change Management.

Louise authored the chapter *Embedding eLearning in Further Education,* which was published in the book *Applied eLearning and eTeaching in HE* in 2008.

I would like to thank my husband for his support through all my academic, professional, and personal pursuits and challenges.

Alex Little is a director and co-founder of Digital Campus (http://digital-campus.org), a not-for-profit company specializing in ICT and educational technologies for emerging countries. Alex spent 18 months working with Voluntary Services Overseas at Mekelle University, Ethiopia, developing the University's eLearning capacities through a teacher training program alongside ICT infrastructure development. Currently based at Alcalá University, Spain, Alex continues to have a close involvement with Mekelle University.

Prior to moving to Mekelle, Alex spent eight years as a senior web developer and researcher for the Open University UK, focused on developing software tools and systems to support distance and online learners. With the OU Knowledge Media Institute, Alex integrated a range of social software tools into the OpenLearn platform.

Visit Alex's blog at http://alexlittle.net.

www.PacktPub.com

Support files, eBooks, discount offers and more

You might want to visit www.PacktPub.com for support files and downloads related to your book.

Did you know that Packt offers eBook versions of every book published, with PDF and ePub files available? You can upgrade to the eBook version at www.PacktPub.com and as a print book customer, you are entitled to a discount on the eBook copy. Get in touch with us at service@packtpub.com for more details.

At www.PacktPub.com, you can also read a collection of free technical articles, sign up for a range of free newsletters and receive exclusive discounts and offers on Packt books and eBooks.

http://PacktLib.PacktPub.com

Do you need instant solutions to your IT questions? PacktLib is Packt's online digital book library. Here, you can access, read and search across Packt's entire library of books.

Why Subscribe?

- ► Fully searchable across every book published by Packt
- ► Copy and paste, print and bookmark content
- ► On demand and accessible via web browser

Free Access for Packt account holders

If you have an account with Packt at www.PacktPub.com, you can use this to access PacktLib today and view nine entirely free books. Simply use your login credentials for immediate access.

Dedicated To
My Son, Nico

Table of Contents

Preface

Moodle 2.0 Multimedia Cookbook provides a plethora of recipes showing you how to manage, link, and embed different multimedia resources into your Moodle course. An ideal choice if you don't have the time to read a long tutorial and want quick ways to enhance your Moodle course.

Go beyond your normal use of Moodle and make your courses really attractive. This cookbook will give you inspiration and teach you to do things you never knew were possible. Link, edit, and embed bitmaps and photographs to illustrate your lessons. Learn to resize and convert images to the most appropriate formats for Moodle courses, interactive documents, and e-portfolios. Work with animated graphics to create engaging activities and learn the most complex topics related to formats, compression, bitmaps, and vector graphics while following steps in these simple recipes.

What this book covers

Chapter 1, Creating Interactive User eXperiences, explains how to create rich activities for our Moodle courses.

Chapter 2, Working with 2D and 3D Maps, illustrates how to create and embed different types of 2D and 3D interactive maps in your Moodle courses. The recipes use Web resources as well as free and open source software to build and display interactive maps.

Chapter 3, Working with Different Types of Interactive Charts, describes how to create and embed different types of 2D and 3D interactive and static charts in Moodle courses. The recipes use diverse tools and techniques to display data in charts and to provide students with the necessary information for their activities.

Chapter 4, Integrating Interactive Documents, explains how to use diverse types of interactive documents in your Moodle courses. The recipes use the most popular free, commercial, Web-based, and desktop-based software to create the interactive documents for Moodle courses and provide students with the necessary information for their research activities.

Chapter 5, Working with Audio, Sound, Music, and Podcasts, describes how to work with different types of audio files to offer sound, music, and podcasts in your Moodle courses. The recipes use diverse tools to record, edit, and convert the different audio files, covering the most common scenarios for multimedia Moodle activities.

Chapter 6, Creating and Integrating Screencasts and Videos, explains how to create screencasts and edit, link, and embed videos for our Moodle courses. The recipes use diverse free and open source multi-platform tools to record, edit, and convert the different video files, covering the most common scenarios for multimedia Moodle activities.

Chapter 7, Working with Bitmaps and Photographs, illustrates how to work with different types of image file formats that use lossless and lossy compression schemes. The recipes use diverse tools to edit, enhance, and convert the different image files, covering the most common scenarios for multimedia Moodle activities.

Chapter 8, Working with Vector Graphics, explains how to work with different types of vector graphics formats. The recipes use diverse free and open source tools to edit, enhance, and convert the different vector graphics files. Vector graphics are one of the most difficult formats to handle in Moodle courses

Chapter 9, Designing and Integrating E-portfolios, illustrates how to design and integrate e-Portfolios in Moodle courses. You will learn exciting techniques to organize your information for your students as well as combine everything learned so far in interactive e-Portfolios.

What you need for this book

You need basic knowledge of Moodle 1.9 or 2.0 and have Moodle installed and ready to be worked on.

Who this book is for

This cookbook is designed for teachers who want to learn how to insert different multimedia assets into their Moodle courses. It is expected that you will have basic knowledge of Moodle 1.9 or 2.0 and have Moodle installed and ready to be worked on. Teachers of different subjects can adapt the recipes to best suit their specific subject.

Conventions

In this book, you will find a number of styles of text that distinguish between different kinds of information. Here are some examples of these styles, and an explanation of their meaning.

Code words in text are shown as follows: "After selecting the pictures, we create a new folder in Windows Explorer, for example, `C:\Images_Traveling`."

A block of code is set as follows:

```
<object type="image/svg+xml" data="http://localhost/draftfile.php/13/
user/draft/168792725/Embed_SVG_Spiral.svg">
</object>
</p>
```

When we wish to draw your attention to a particular part of a code block, the relevant lines or items are set in bold:

```
<p><a href="http://localhost/draftfile.php/13/user/draft/168792725/
Embed_SVG_Spiral.svg">Define this.</a></p>
<p>What is it?</p>
<p>Where can you find it?</p>
<p> </p>
<p>
```

New terms and **important words** are shown in bold. Words that you see on the screen, in menus or dialog boxes for example, appear in the text like this: "Click on **Add | Photo**."

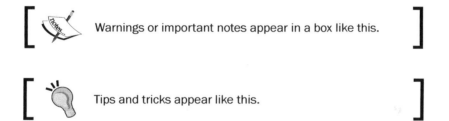

Warnings or important notes appear in a box like this.

Tips and tricks appear like this.

Reader feedback

Feedback from our readers is always welcome. Let us know what you think about this book—what you liked or may have disliked. Reader feedback is important for us to develop titles that you really get the most out of.

To send us general feedback, simply send an e-mail to feedback@packtpub.com, and mention the book title via the subject of your message.

If there is a book that you need and would like to see us publish, please send us a note in the **SUGGEST A TITLE** form on www.packtpub.com or e-mail suggest@packtpub.com.

If there is a topic that you have expertise in and you are interested in either writing or contributing to a book, see our author guide on www.packtpub.com/authors.

Customer support

Now that you are the proud owner of a Packt book, we have a number of things to help you to get the most from your purchase.

Errata

Although we have taken every care to ensure the accuracy of our content, mistakes do happen. If you find a mistake in one of our books—maybe a mistake in the text or the code—we would be grateful if you would report this to us. By doing so, you can save other readers from frustration and help us improve subsequent versions of this book. If you find any errata, please report them by visiting http://www.packtpub.com/support, selecting your book, clicking on the **errata submission form** link, and entering the details of your errata. Once your errata are verified, your submission will be accepted and the errata will be uploaded on our website, or added to any list of existing errata, under the Errata section of that title. Any existing errata can be viewed by selecting your title from http://www.packtpub.com/support.

Piracy

Piracy of copyright material on the Internet is an ongoing problem across all media. At Packt, we take the protection of our copyright and licenses very seriously. If you come across any illegal copies of our works, in any form, on the Internet, please provide us with the location address or website name immediately so that we can pursue a remedy.

Please contact us at copyright@packtpub.com with a link to the suspected pirated material.

We appreciate your help in protecting our authors, and our ability to bring you valuable content.

Questions

You can contact us at questions@packtpub.com if you are having a problem with any aspect of the book, and we will do our best to address it.

1
Creating Interactive User eXperiences

In this chapter, we will cover:

- ▶ Creating a cloze with pictures
- ▶ Designing a True or False quiz
- ▶ Developing a quandary maze activity with images
- ▶ Carrying out and embedding an interactive flowchart
- ▶ Designing matching activities with pictures
- ▶ Ordering paragraphs with related scenes
- ▶ Linking external 2D interactive activities
- ▶ Linking external 3D interactive activities

Introduction

There are many ways to build or create rich interactive User eXperiences. We are going to learn how to design them using a combination of technologies, free and open source software, as well as services available on the Web.

This chapter explains how to create rich activities for Moodle courses. We will work with graphics to create engaging activities for our students. Images tend to be an important asset to bear in mind when designing an activity.

The aim of this chapter is to insert in our Moodle course the available applications in Web 2.0 in order to enrich our activities. We will use Hot Potatoes, JClic, and Quandary 2, which are visually rich, free software available on the Web. You can design activities using interactive websites as well.

This book will cover the topics of general knowledge. Therefore, in each chapter, we will cover a different topic. This chapter deals with Nobel Prize winners and people of achievement.

Creating a cloze with pictures

In this activity, we are going to create a cloze activity with images. We will deal with a Nobel Prize winner and write the biography using some images. Students write the correct name for those images and afterwards they name the person. The idea is that the images are to be relevant to both the biography and the work carried out by this Nobel Prize winner. By the way, you are not going to be given the name of the person until the end of this activity!

Getting ready

In this activity, we will use Hot Potatoes to create an activity using JCloze. You can download Hot Potatoes software from its website: `http://hotpot.uvic.ca/#downloads`.

 Hot Potatoes is a freeware, whose suite includes six applications enabling you to create interactive multiple-choice, short-answer, jumbled-sentence, crossword, matching/ordering, and gap-fill exercises for the World Wide Web.

How to do it...

First of all, choose the person that you want to write about. You can choose a Nobel Prize winner from the following website: `http://nobelprize.org/`. Then, read the biography (you can find a more detailed biography at the following website: `http://www.famouspeoplebiographyguide.com`) and design the gap-filling exercise.

We design the activity in such a way that students are to be given the clue in the form of a picture placed near a textbox, where they have to write the correct word. Therefore, we have to find pictures in order to design the activity. Look for the free clipart at the Office Online Clip Art & Media at the following website: `http://office.microsoft.com/en-us/images/`; another interesting and suitable website is `http://www.openclipart.org/`. Follow these steps in order to create a folder and find images for the activity:

1. Create a new folder in Windows Explorer, for example `C:\Images_Nobelprize`.

2. Open your web browser to search for an appropriate image.

3. Write the word **BABY** in the textbox and click on the search button, as shown in the following screenshot:

4. Double-click on the desired clipart or picture. The picture will appear in another bigger window.

5. Right-click on the image and click on **Save Picture As...**, as shown in the following screenshot:

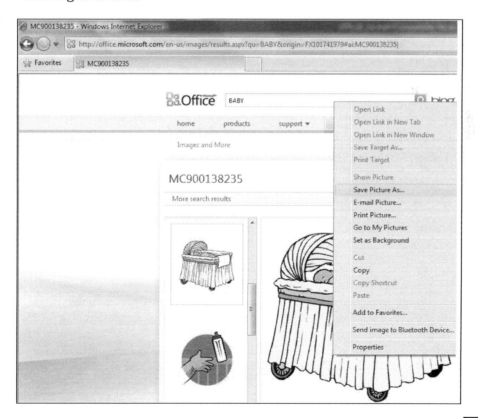

6. Save the picture in the folder that was created in step 1. Choose the **JPEG** extension, as shown in the following screenshot:

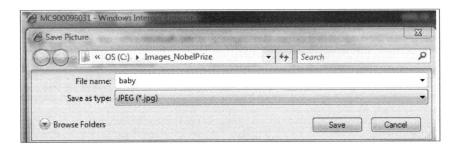

9. Repeat steps 2 – 6 in order to look for more images relevant to the biography of the person chosen.

How it works...

Run the Hot Potatoes software and click on **JCloze** (the blue potato). Follow these steps in order to design the activity:

1. Complete the **Title** block.

2. Write the biography of the person. Highlight the word where you want to create a gap.

3. Click on **Gap** when you want to add one, as shown in the following screenshot:

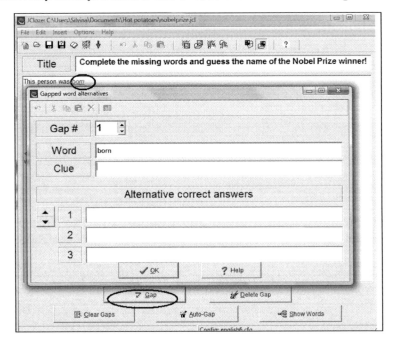

4. The circled underlined word is the one that is to be missing in the activity.

5. You can add clues if you want or any alternative words. Then click on **OK**.

6. Click on **File | Save** and save the file in the folder that was created to save the images.

7. Insert the image to give a visual clue to the gap. Position the cursor where you want to insert the image. Click on **Insert | Picture | Picture from Local File**, as shown in the following screenshot:

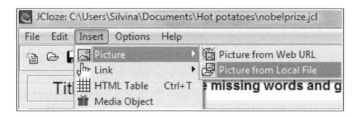

8. Choose the picture that you want to insert, click on **Open**, and then click **OK**. You will not see the image, but you will see HTML code in the textbox.

9. Click on **File | Create Web Page | Standard Format**. Click on **Save**. Click on **View the exercise in my browser**. You will see the activity, as shown in the following screenshot:

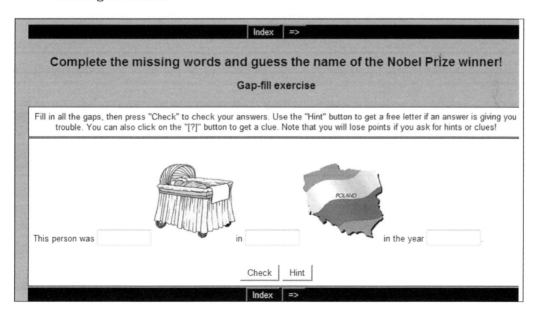

This is just a part of the cloze. Add more images giving more clues about the correct Nobel Prize winner.

There's more

Now upload the previous activity designed in Hot Potatoes in our Moodle course. Open your Moodle course and choose the weekly outline section where the activity needs to be inserted. Before uploading the activity in Moodle, install the Hot Potatoes module in Moodle 2. So, if you do not have it installed, you need to talk to the administrator to do so. By the way, do you know who the Nobel Prize winner is?

Uploading the activity in Moodle

To upload both the activity and the images used in Hot Potatoes to our Moodle course, follow these steps:

1. Click on **Add an activity | HotPot**.
2. Click on the downwards arrow in the **Name** block and choose **Get from source file**.
3. Click on **Add | Upload a file | Browse |** look for the file that you want to upload and click on it and on **Open | Upload this file**.
4. Repeat step 2 in order to upload the images to the Moodle course used in the Hot Potatoes activity.
5. In the **Display** block, click on the downwards arrow in **Navigation** and choose **Embedded web page**.
6. Click on **Save and display**. The activity looks as shown in the following screenshot:

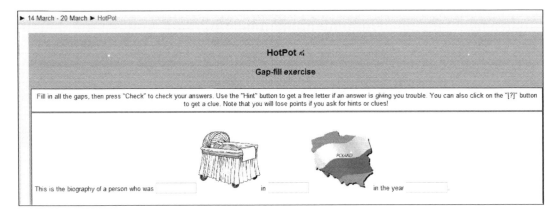

Designing a True or False quiz

In this activity, we are going to design a True or False quiz. It is not an ordinary one though. We create a guessing activity in which students decide whether the answers are either True or False, and in that way they try to guess the name of the Nobel Prize winner once again! So, let's get ready.

Getting ready

Choose the Nobel Prize winner that we want our students to guess. Then, design the activity using Moodle and insert images into our course, which is to be the multimedia asset in this recipe. We are also going to design the same activity using Hot Potatoes JQuiz (the yellow potato).

How to do it...

Bear in mind what type of information we want our students to guess. We are going to insert images in the questions. So, in this case, use free clipart from the following website: `http://www.free-clipart-pictures.net`.

Choose the weekly outline section where we want to insert our activity and follow these steps:

1. Click on **Add an activity | Quiz**.
2. Complete the **Name** and the **Introduction** block.
3. Click on **Save and display**.
4. Click on **Show**, as shown in the following screenshot:

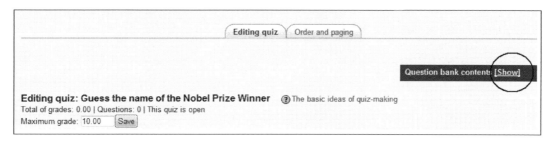

5. Click on **Create a new question....**

6. A pop-out window displaying different types of questions will appear. Choose **True/False**, as shown in the following screenshot:

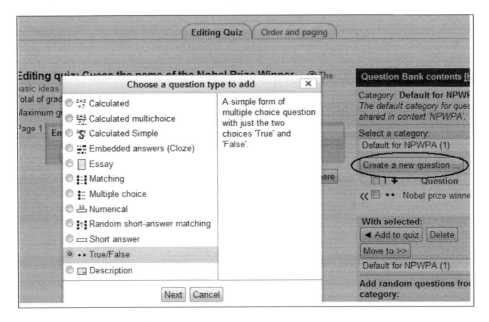

7. Click on **Next**.

8. Complete the **Question text** block. You can start adding information to students such as 'This person is a man'.

9. Open your web browser and enter the following website: http://www.free-clipart-pictures.net.

10. Click on **Child Clipart**.

11. Right-click on the chosen clipart and click on **Properties**, as shown in the following screenshot:

12. There will appear a pop-out window with the URL address of the image, to highlight it, and then right-click and copy it, as shown in the following screenshot:

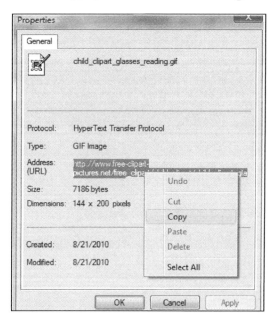

13. Click on **OK**.

14. Go back to our Moodle course. Click on the **Insert/edit image** icon to upload the previous image.

15. Complete the pop-up window, as shown in the following screenshot:

16. Click on **Insert**.

17. Complete the **Feedback for the response 'True'** and **Feedback for the response 'False'** blocks. You can add the correct images instead of writing. For example, if the person is not a woman, insert the image of a girl and a cross; if the person is a man, insert the image of the boy with a tick.

18. Click on **Save changes**.

19. Click on **Add a question...** | **True or False** | **Next**, as shown in the following screenshot:

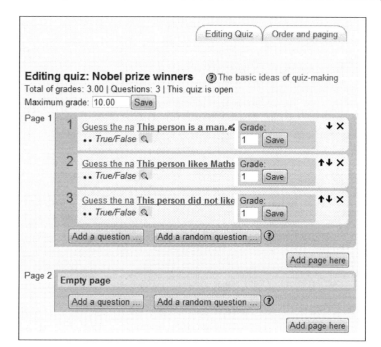

20. Complete the blocks with information about the Nobel Prize winner.

21. Add as many questions as necessary.

22. When there is no need to add more questions, go back to the course. The activity is ready to work with!

How it works...

Students are going to attempt the True or False quiz and after getting the results of the clues, they have to guess the name of the Nobel Prize winner. You may supply the name of the person in the last question of the activity. By the way, in this case, the Nobel Prize winner is John F. Nash Jr.

You can also save the images in a folder, as we have done in the previous recipe.

There's more...

We can also design the same activity using Hot Potatoes. This software also allows us to design True/False quizzes. Therefore, we open Hot Potatoes and we click on **JQuiz**. To start designing the guessing activity, follow these steps:

1. Complete the **Title** block.

2. Choose **Multiple-choice** in the downwards arrow that appears on the top right-hand margin.

3. Write the sentence that students have to guess in the **Q1** block.

4. Write **True** and click on **Accept as correct** within **Settings**.

5. Write **False** on the next one, as shown in the following screenshot:

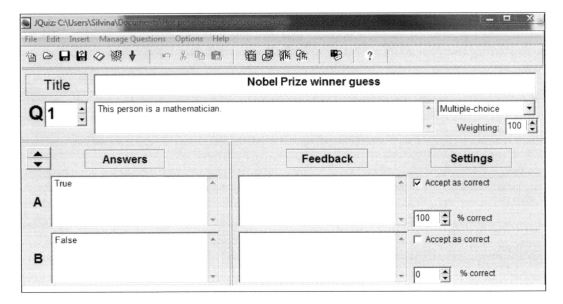

6. Click on the downwards arrow next to **Q1**, and **Q2** will appear. Go on adding sentences to give tips to your students.

7. Save the file. Click on **File | Create a web page | Standard Format | Save | View the exercise in my browser**.

8. You can also add any images to the activity following the steps in the previous recipe.

9. Upload the activity in the Moodle course, as explained in the previous recipe.

More info

We can also design a True or False activity using `http://testmoz.com/`. It is an interactive webpage where you can easily design this quiz. We can upload this activity in our Moodle course using the **Add a resource** choice. The website corrects the quiz by itself.

Follow these steps to create an interactive True or False quiz using testmoz:

1. Click on **Make a test**.
2. Complete the **Test name** block.
3. Write a password. Then click on **Continue**.
4. Click on **Settings** and complete the settings blocks. Then click on **Save**.
5. Click on **Add a New Question**.
6. Click on the downwards arrow in **Type** and choose **True/False**. Write the question in the **Question** block.
7. Click on **Save and Add a New Question**, as shown in the following screenshot:

8. When you finish adding questions, click on **Save | Publish | Publish**.
9. Go back to the Moodle course to upload the quiz. Click on **Add a resource | URL**.
10. Complete the **Name** and **Description** blocks. Remember to write the password, otherwise students won't be able to work with the quiz.

11. Copy and paste the URL of the quiz in the **External URL** block.

12. Click on **Save and return to course**.

13. The quiz will be within our Moodle course!

 We should bear in mind that the quiz results from testmoz won't get passed back to Moodle, therefore they won't be included in the students' grade book.

See also

▶ *Creating a cloze with pictures.*

Developing a quandary maze activity with images

In this activity, we are going to create a quandary maze using Quandary 2, which is a free and open source software. The only disadvantage is that it is only available for Windows. You can download it from the following website: `http://www.halfbakedsoftware.com/quandary.php`.

The quandary maze is about two people of achievement and a special animal. The three of them share a common characteristic. Students should guess their names by the clues given, and at the end of the maze they are going to figure out who they are. The idea is that they do not know who they are until the end of the maze in order to keep the mystery.

Getting ready

First of all, download and install Quandary 2. Then, think of the two people of achievement and the animal who share a common characteristic. Therefore, some information can be shared in the quandary maze, and in some instances, share the decision points or go back to them.

We will upload images in this activity, so create a new folder in your default web browser, for example, `C:\Images_PeopleofAchievement`. Save all the images here that we choose to design our activity.

How to do it...

Open Quandary 2. The title of the activity is: People of Achievement and a Special Animal. Students choose different decision points, and they will have to guess whose biography they are reading. They are provided with different clues, both by text and images.

Go to http://commons.wikimedia.org, wherein there are many free clipart to work with. Search for images that we want to insert in the activity and save them in the folder that we have already created.

Open Quandary 2 and follow these steps in order to develop this activity:

1. Create a folder to save both the file and the images to work with.
2. Click on **File** and select **New**.
3. Click on **File | Save as**. Save the file in the folder that was just created.
4. Complete the **Exercise Title** block.
5. Complete the **Decision Point title** block.
6. Complete the **Decision Point contents** block.
7. Click on **New Link**, and click on the drop-down box in the pop-out window and select **Create a new decision point**.
8. Complete the new block. Click on **OK**.
9. Place the cursor in the **Link text** block and click on the **Insert a picture** icon. Click on **Picture from local file**, as shown in the following screenshot:

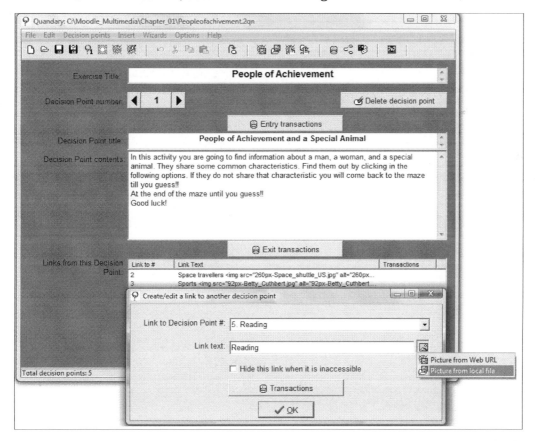

10. Browse for the picture within the folder that you have created. Click on **Open | OK | OK**.

11. Insert two or more **New Links** in the same way. Therefore, repeat steps 7-10 in order to create more decision points.

12. Click on the right arrow on the left-hand side of the margin **Decision Point number** and the number changes to number 2. Go over the same process for making the maze, while guiding the students as to who they are.

13. When you finish, click on **File | Save File**.

14. Click on **File** and select **Export to XHTML**.

How it works...

It is time to upload the quandary activity into Moodle. Upload the activity as if it were a Hot Potatoes activity, so we need to have the HotPot module for this activity as well. Select the weekly outline section where you want to place the activity and follow these steps:

1. Click on **Add an activity | HotPot**.

2. Click on the downwards arrow in the **Name** block and choose **Get from source file**.

3. Click on **Add | Upload a file | Browse |** look for the file that you want to upload and click on it and on **Open | Upload this file**.

4. Repeat step 2 in order to upload the images to the Moodle course used in the Hot Potatoes activity.

5. In the **Display** block, click on the downwards arrow in **Navigation** and choose **Embedded web page**.

6. Click on **Save and display**; the activity looks as shown in the following screenshot:

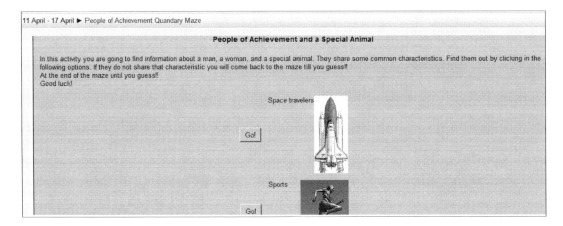

By the way, their names are Valentina Vladimirovna Tereshkova, Yuri Alekseyevich Gagarin, and Laika, the first dog in space.

Carrying out and embedding an interactive flowchart

In this recipe, we are going to work with the following website: `http://classtools.net`. There is a new item within its incredible variation of interactive activities and games that we can develop for free—**Telescopic Topic** allows us to carry out an interactive flowchart that can be opened as far as we want to expand our reading. The idea is to choose a Nobel Prize winner and write his biography; students can expand it, depending on how much they want to read.

You could give the name of the Nobel Prize winner at the beginning of the activity or you could play another type of guessing game, and after they read the biography of the said person, they have to find out who the person is.

Getting ready

First of all, think about the person to write about. After that, go to the aforementioned website and choose **Telescopic Topic** generator.

I would like to point out that this website offers an upgrade version with more facilities to work with. This is optional, and the recipe that we are going to work with is available for free.

How to do it...

You should think of the main items that will expand in the biography and add additional data to it.

We can either design this in any type of writing processor, that is to say Microsoft Word or Open Office, copy-and-paste it in the **Telescopic Topic** generator, or write it directly in the website. In this case, the activity is carried out directly in the website.

Follow these steps in order to develop the activity:

1. Write the bullets for the biography of the person, as shown in the following screenshot:

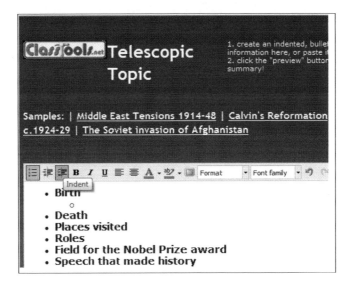

2. After writing the main bullets, click on the **Indent** icon, as shown in the previous screenshot, to add data on those items.

3. Go on and complete the flowchart, indent the information towards the right. If you want to go back, choose the arrow towards the left.

4. Make a link to a famous speech by this person. Highlight the words that you want students to click on, in the link. Click on the **Insert/edit a link** icon.

5. Complete the **Insert/edit a link** block, which will appear in a pop-up window, as shown in the following screenshot:

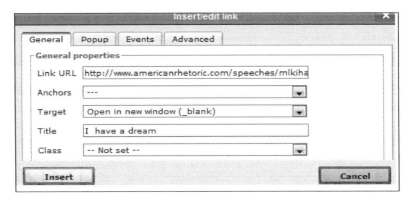

6. Click on **Insert**.

7. Click on **Preview**.

8. Click on **Save**.

9. Enter a password and click on **Submit**.

10. Click on **embed**, on the top left-hand margin and copy the code. You will use it afterwards to insert it in our Moodle course.

How it works...

We will carry out this activity in **Online text** so that students can say who the person is and why using the speech that we have made links to, they have a special clue. Follow these steps so that you can design the activity:

1. Click on **Add an activity | Online text** (within **Assignments**).

2. Complete the **Assignment name** block.

3. Complete the **Description** block.

4. Click on the **HTML Source Editor** icon and copy the code that is copied from the website.

5. Click on **Update**.

6. Click on **Save and return to course**.

7. The activity looks as shown in the following screenshot:

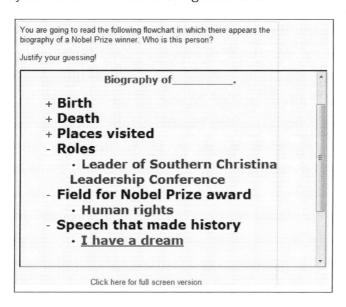

By the way, the name of the Nobel Prize winner is Martin Luther King Jr.

Designing matching activities with images

In this activity, we would be working with another application available on the Web. It is a free, open source software called JClic author 0.2.0.5. So, the first thing that we have to do is to install it. We will create a matching activity with images. You can also carry out this activity using either Moodle or JMatch within Hot Potatoes.

Choose 16 people of achievement and their main characteristic will be labeled by an icon image. So, the students have to match each person with the achievement that they are famous for. Can you think of so many talented persons! Let's get ready!

Getting ready

We are going to work with JClic author, but in case that you do not happen to have it installed, you can download it from the following website: `http://clic.xtec.cat/en/jclic/download.htm`. You have to click on the **JClic author** icon and download the software following the steps.

After the installation, we are going to work with images from the following website: `http://commons.wikimedia.org`. Create a folder (as we have already done in the previous activities), in which we save all the icon images that we have chosen that represent these special people.

How to do it...

These are the steps that you have to follow to design the activity:

1. Open the JClic author. Select **File | New Project** and complete the pop-up window, as shown in the following screenshot:

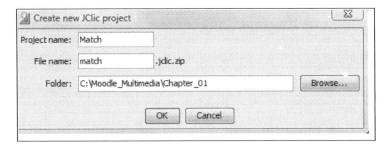

2. Save the activity in the folder that you have created and saved the images in. Then click **OK**.

3. Click on **Project** and complete the **Title** and the **Description** blocks, writing what students have to do in this activity.

4. Click on **Activities** and select **Insert | New activity**. Select **Complex association**, as shown in the following screenshot:

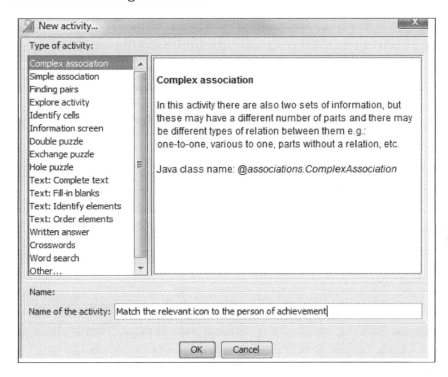

5. Write the name of the activity, as shown in the previous screenshot. Then click on **OK**.

6. Complete the blocks related to **Options**, as you want to display the activity.

7. Then click on **Window**. You are also going to customize it yourself or keep it as it is. There are many options to work with.

8. You can also choose to design the messages by clicking on **Messages**.

9. Click on **Panel**. **Grid A** is the grid on the left, and write the names of the people of achievement. **Grid B** is the grid on the right used to insert the icon images.

10. Click on **Grid A** and complete the options, as shown in the following screenshot. Therefore, you can insert 16 names by clicking in each cell and completing the pop-out window that appears for each of them. Only enter text on this grid:

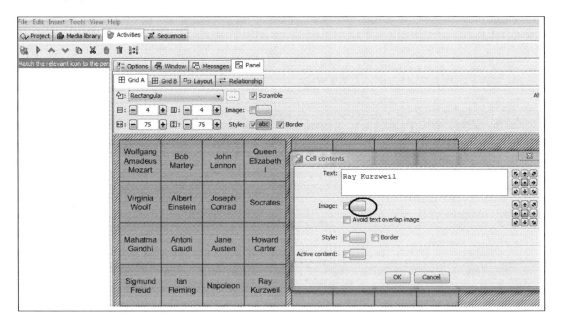

11. Click on **Grid B**. Click on a cell, and then click on the big rectangle next to **Image**, as shown circled in the previous screenshot.

12. A new pop-out window will appear. Click on **New media object....** Choose the image that you want to upload. Click on **Open | OK | OK**. The image will appear inside the cell.

13. Repeat the same process 15 more times, because we have inserted 16 people of achievement! Another option is to choose less items to connect.

14. Select **File | Save** to save the changes made.

15. Choose **View | Preview activity**. You can work out the activity, can't you?

How it works...

Now that we have designed the activity in JClic author, insert the previously created activity in our Moodle course. There is not a module or block available in Moodle 2 to insert JClic activities, and this is the reason why we have to make a link to the said file. Follow these steps to prepare the activity in order to upload it to Moodle afterwards:

1. Click on **Tools** | **Create web page**, as shown in the following screenshot:

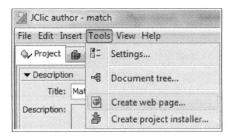

2. A pop-up window appears. Click on **OK** | **Save** | **Yes**.

3. The activity is ready to work with. It is time to upload it to the Moodle course.

Add this matching activity as a resource in the course. It can be the warm up activity to the introduction of any topic to deal with. Therefore, choose the weekly outline section where you want to place the activity and follow these steps:

1. Click on **Add a resource** | **File**.

2. Complete the **Name** and **Description** blocks.

3. Click on **Add** | **Upload a file** | **Browse** and look for the file to upload in Moodle. Look for the **.htm** file that was previously created.

4. Click on **Open** | **Upload this file**.

5. Repeat steps 3 and 4 to upload the `.jclic.zip` file as well, as shown in the following screenshot:

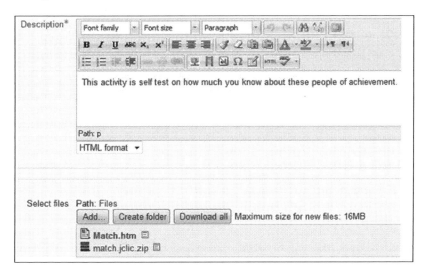

6. Click on **Save and display**. The JClic activity is ready to work with within Moodle!

There's more

We can add another activity after this one. Use this matching activity as a lead to a writing one, for example, or as a warm up for a special assignment. We can add an **Online text** activity so that students give their reasons on who the most amazing person is and why; for instance.

Creating a writing activity

Create a writing activity using the previous one designed in JClic author as a pre-writing one. Thus, follow these steps to insert this new one in our Moodle course:

1. Click on **Add an activity | Upload a single file**.

2. Complete the **Assignment name** and **Description** blocks.

3. Click on **Save and return to course**.

Ordering paragraphs with related scenes

We can design this type of activity using several external software or tools available in Web 2.0. You can use JMatch within Hot Potatoes or a matching activity within the JClic author. However, we are not going to use those because we have already used them in the earlier recipes. Therefore, design an interactive timeline using the following website: `http://www.readwritethink.org/classroom-resources/student-interactives/timeline-30007.html` or you can also design it using Microsoft Word or Open Office with images in it.

Getting ready

Enter the aforementioned website and click on **Timeline Tool** so that we can design the timeline of a Nobel Prize winner. By the way, can you guess who we are going to work with?

How to do it...

Another screen will appear displaying the type of timeline that we are going to develop. So, these are the steps to follow:

1. Click on **Get Started**.

2. Another pop-up window will appear in which you have to complete the **Title** block as well as the author of the timeline in the **By** block.

3. Click on **Choose | Event** within **Unit of Measure**.

4. Click on **Next Entry** on the top-right margin.

5. Complete the **Event**, **Title**, and **Description** blocks.

6. Click on **Next Entry** on the top-right margin as many times as the number of events you want to add.

7. When you finish the timeline, click on the *Print Screen* key and then paste the image in the Paint software or something similar.

8. Click on the **Select** icon and cut the timeline. Copy-and-paste it in a new document and save it as a `.png` file so that we can upload it in our Moodle course. The timeline looks as shown in the following screenshot:

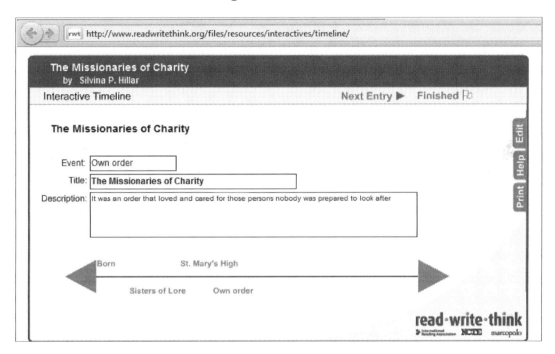

How it works...

We have already designed a timeline using the website. We have done it using the names of the events relevant to what this famous person has achieved throughout life. Thus, students are to be given several paragraphs and they have to put them in order using the information in this timeline.

Design this activity using **Upload a single file** because the main object is that they write the paragraphs in order of adding as much information as possible. Therefore, these are the steps that you have to follow to design this activity:

1. Click on **Add an activity | Upload a single file**.

2. Complete the **Assignment name** and **Description** blocks.

3. Click on the **Insert / edit an Image** icon | **Find or upload an image** |**Upload a file** (on the left-hand margin) |**Browse**.

4. When you find the image, click on **Open** | **Upload this file** | **Insert** | **OK**.

5. Click on **Save and return to course**.

By the way, the name of the Nobel Prize winner is Mother Teresa.

Linking external 2D interactive activities

In this activity, we will write a brief introduction of the mathematician who worked out a theorem of triangles. Afterwards, we will make a link to an interactive blog that allows students to open a file and complete a chart about different 2D shapes. Thus, let's get ready.

Getting ready

This recipe is different from the others because, in this case, we will work with the results of people of achievement. Students read about him and they do an activity.

Look for some information about an old mathematician who worked out the theorem of triangles. Make a link to an interactive website that explains this theorem in an attractive way and then work with 2D shapes. We can design the activity in two parts. The first part is a passive activity because we have to give students some information about 2D shapes. Thus, add a resource, a page, and the second part is the activity.

Design the activity in **Upload a single file**, because the website that we choose to work with has a file that students have to complete. Therefore, when they complete it, they can submit it to the course!

How to do it...

The activity has already been explained before. Choose the weekly outline section where we want to place the resource. Then, follow these steps in order to carry it out:

1. Click on **Add a resource** | **Page**.

2. Complete the **Name** block.

3. Complete the **Description** block.

4. Complete the **Page content** block and make a link to the following websites: `http://www-history.mcs.st-and.ac.uk/Biographies/Pythagoras.html` and `http://www.mathsisfun.com/pythagoras.html`, as shown in the following screenshot:

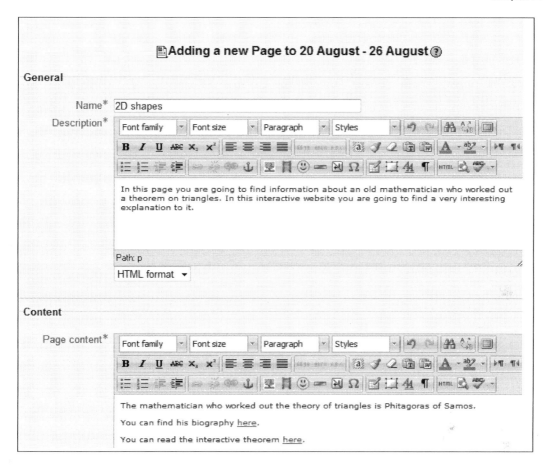

5. Click on **Save and return to course**.

How it works...

We have already added some passive material in our course and now we add the activity in our Moodle course, just after the resource. So, follow these steps to design the activity:

1. Click on **Add an activity | Upload a single file**, within **Assignments**.

2. Complete the **Assignment name** block.

3. Complete the **Description** block and make a link to the following blog: `http://www.bgfl.org/bgfl/custom/resources_ftp/client_ftp/ks2/maths/3d/index.htm`.

4. Click on **Save and return to course**.

5. The activity looks as shown in the following screenshot:

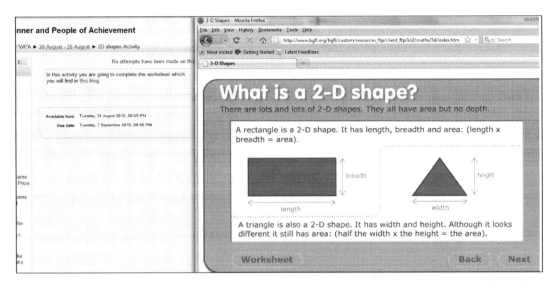

Linking external 3D interactive activities

In this activity, we are going to write a brief introduction of the mathematician who is known to be the Father of Geometry. Afterwards, we make a link to the previous interactive blog that allows students to open a file and complete a chart about different 3D shapes.

Getting ready

This recipe is similar to the previous one. Look for some information about an old mathematician who is considered the Father of Sacred Geometry. The first part is a passive activity because we give students some information about Euclid of Alexandria.

Design the activity in **Upload a single file**, because the website that we choose to work with has a file that students have to complete. Therefore, when they complete it, they can submit it to the Moodle course!

How to do it...

The activity has already been explained before. Choose the weekly outline section where you want to place the resource. Then, follow these steps in order to carry it out:

1. Click on **Add a resource | Page**.

2. Complete the **Name** block.

3. Complete the **Description** block.

4. Complete the **Page content** block and make a link to the following website: `http://concentricclothing.com/blog-post/sacred-geometry/euclid-the-father-of-geometry-sacred-geometry`.

5. Click on **Save and return to course**.

How it works...

Add the activity in the same weekly outline section, just after the resource. Follow these steps to design the activity:

1. Click on **Add an activity | Upload a single file**, within **Assignments**.

2. Complete the **Assignment name** block.

3. Complete the **Description** block and make a link to the following blog: `http://www.bgfl.org/bgfl/custom/resources_ftp/client_ftp/ks2/maths/3d/index.htm`.

4. Click on **Save and return to course**.

5. The activity looks as shown in the following screenshot:

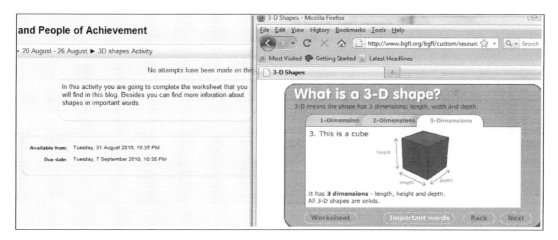

There's more...

We have added a mathematical activity, but we can also add a link to the following website in which students can design a plane by dragging and dropping different 3D shapes: `http://airplaneassembly.webs.com/`. They can learn about aeroplane parts and recognize the geometric shapes used in making them.

2
Working with 2D and 3D Maps

In this chapter, we will cover:

- ► Creating maps with sceneries
- ► Drawing regions within a map
- ► Labeling a map with pins
- ► Drawing 3D maps using Bing Maps
- ► Drawing 3D maps using 3DVIA Shape for Maps
- ► Using Google maps to locate European bridges
- ► Displaying interactive information about the solar system
- ► Working with constellation maps
- ► Embedding a map of Mars
- ► Labeling the moon
- ► Watching the universe

Introduction

This chapter explains how to create and embed different types of either 2D or 3D interactive maps in our Moodle courses. The creation of these maps will be done using resources available in the Web 2.0 as well as the free and open source software. Thanks to these amazing tools, we can design and display interactive maps in our Moodle courses.

Whenever you think of a map, you may either think of the traditional planisphere or the terrestrial globe. There are several types of maps apart from those previously mentioned. We can work with maps of the moon, Mars, constellations, and even the universe! Thus, we are not only going to focus on our planet, but we are going to travel even further!

Taking into account that this book covers the topic of general knowledge, the topic of this chapter is going to deal with **Traveling Around the World and Watching the Universe**. After reading this chapter, you can focus on your next holiday!

We explain how to work with different types of maps. We are going to be as creative as possible. We should try to work with maps in an unconventional way. That is to say, the idea is to use a map for a Geography class, but we can use maps as a resource for any type of activity. Thus, we can work with the Geography teacher and he/she could work on another geographical feature of the place that we are working with. Therefore, in that way, we are adding more information to the place we are exploring.

Maps are very attractive and they may become quite appealing to our students as long as we find a way to develop a rich activity using them. We should encourage the use of maps and the available resources that we have on the Web so that they can insert them in their homework by themselves as well. Thus, we can develop the activities in such a way that we can either provide the map or ask them to design a map.

We can also work with maps in the case of Literature. We can ask students to draw a map of a place that has never existed in the real world, though it did in a story. Thus, another bit of homework that could prove helpful would be for students to design and carry out the map of such a place using the tools that we are going to explore in the following recipes. An example of this could be to draw the map of the country Ruritania and locate the cities of Zenda and Strealsau. These places do not exist in the real world, but they exist in the book *The Prisoner of Zenda* by *Anthony Hope*. So, many things can be done with maps.

Creating maps with sceneries

In this activity, we are going to create a map with sceneries. Therefore, we could either browse our files for pictures from our trips or holidays, or we can search for sceneries on the Web. After selecting the pictures, we create a new folder in Windows Explorer, for example `C:\Images_Traveling`. In this folder, we save all the pictures so as to organize our work.

We will use the following well-known website: `http://earth.google.com/` to design a map using the pictures we have saved in the folder that we have just created. Let's get ready!

Getting ready

In this activity, we will work with the previously mentioned website. Therefore, we need to open the web browser and enter it. Click on **Download Google Earth 6**. Read the **Google Maps/ Earth Terms of Service** and if you agree, click on **Agree and Download**. The icon of Google Earth will appear on your desktop, as shown in the following screenshot:

How to do it...

We have already carried out the first steps for this activity. Now, we have to design the maps with the pictures that we want to add. There are also some pictures that are available in the maps; you can also work with them, though the aim of this activity is to upload images in the map. Follow these steps in order to create a folder and find images for the activity:

1. Click on the icon on your desktop and open **Google Earth**.

2. Bring the Earth closer with the icons on the right. Locate a remote city in the southern hemisphere, as shown in the following screenshot:

3. In the **Fly to** block, write "Mar del Plata", or any other remote city. Then press *Enter* or click on the magnifying glass next to the block.

4. You will travel virtually to the desired city. Bring the map forward and locate the place where the picture to be uploaded was taken.

5. Click on **Add | Photo**.

6. Complete the **Name** block.

7. Click on **Browse**. Search for the picture that you want to upload and click on it.

8. Complete the other blocks: **Description | View | Photo**.

9. Click on **OK**.

10. The picture will appear, as shown in the following screenshot:

11. You can repeat the same process as many times as the number of pictures you want to upload.

12. After uploading all the pictures, click on **File | Save | Save Image**, as shown in the following screenshot:

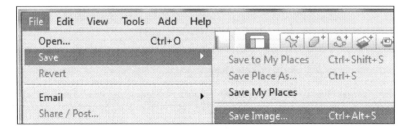

13. Complete the **File name** block and click on **Save**.

How it works...

After uploading the desired pictures to the map, we can create an activity. We could start this course with a little social interaction. We ask our students to think about what element they shouldn't forget if they happen to go to this place. They may not know this city, for sure, unless they live nearby. This is the most interesting part of inserting a remote city that they may want to know more about it! Therefore, a **Chat** is a good idea to have where all the students will be invited in order to discuss the city.

We upload the map that we have created with the images to our activity within the Moodle course. Choose the weekly outline section where you want to insert this activity and follow these steps:

1. Click on **Add an activity | Chat**.
2. Complete the **Name of this chat room** and **Introduction text** blocks.
3. Click on the **Insert/edit image** icon | **Find or upload an image** | **Browse** and look for the image that we have just saved.
4. Click on **Upload this file**.
5. Complete the **Image description** block and click on **Insert**.
6. Click on **Save and return to course**. The activity looks as shown in the following screenshot:

Drawing regions within a map

In this activity, we are going to use an interactive website in which we choose a map to work with. It is a very simple one, but we could enhance it by adding interesting ingredients to the recipe. We will use a software for drawing a region on the map, and highlight a region for our students to work with. As it was pointed out before, we are not going to focus on geographical features, though you can add this ingredient yourself when designing the activity.

Getting ready

We open our default web browser and work with the following website: http://www.fusioncharts.com/maps/Default.asp. We click on **Map Gallery** and choose a map to work with. In this case, we choose a map of the world and highlight five regions, one for each continent. You can modify it and work with different regions within a continent or a country too.

How to do it...

We look for the desired map. We can find different types of maps to work with. Everything depends on what type of activity we have in mind. In this case, as the topic of this chapter has to do with traveling, we circle five regions and ask our students to choose where they would like to go. First of all, we have to find the map and save it as an image so that we can draw the regions and upload it to our Moodle course. Therefore, follow these steps:

1. Click on **click here | World Map with countries** on the aforementioned site.

2. Another pop-up window appears, displaying a map of the world with the countries. There appears a **Map Configuration** block where you can customize some features, as shown in the next screenshot.

3. Click on **Save Map as Image**, as shown in the following screenshot:

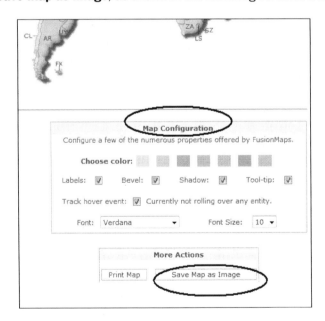

4. Another pop-up window will appear. Click on **Save**.

5. Complete the **File name** block.

6. Click on **Save**.

7. Click on **Open**.

8. A pop-up window displaying the map will appear. Click on **File | Copy**.

9. Paste the map in Paint or Inkscape. Click on **Edit | Paste from** and browse for the name of the file.

10. Select the file and click on **Open**.

11. Use the resources available to draw the regions that you want students to work with, as shown in the following screenshot:

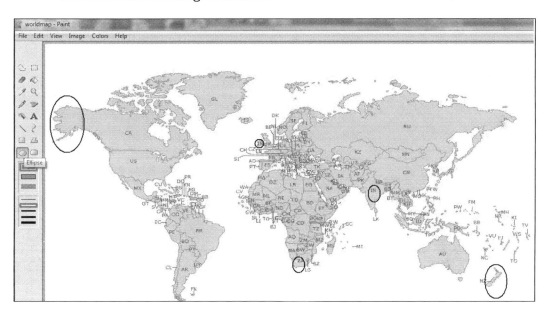

12. Click on **File | Save as** and write a name for the file.

13. Click on **Save**.

How it works...

We have already drawn the regions that we want our students to work with. We have chosen one country from every continent; you can choose another or design it in a different way. We can add a writing activity in which students choose where they would like to travel using the previous map.

Select the weekly outline section where you want to add the activity and follow these steps:

1. Click on **Add an activity | Upload a single file** within **Assignments**.

2. Complete the **Assignment name** and **Description** blocks.

3. Click on the **Insert/edit image** icon | **Find or upload an image** | **Browse**.

4. When you find the image that you want to upload, click on **Open** | **Upload this file**.

5. Complete the **Image description** block.

6. Click on **Insert**.

7. Click on **Save and return to course**. The activity is ready!

8. When students click on the activity, it looks as shown in the following screenshot:

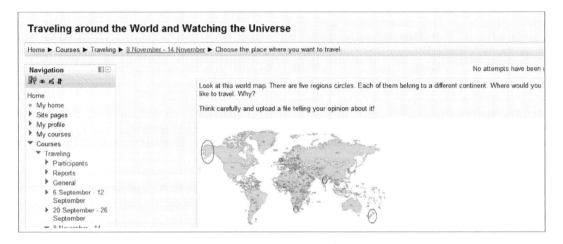

Labeling a map with pins

In this recipe, we will learn how to insert a map in our Moodle course labeled with pins, because we pin all the cities that we are going to work with. Therefore, we insert the map as a resource. After that, we design activities for our students to use the interactive map that we have just added. It is another way to use a resource, making our Moodle course more appealing to the eyes of our students.

Getting ready

We are going to work with Google Earth, as we did in the first recipe, so we have already installed it. We should think of the cities to insert in our course because we need to pin them all!

How to do it...

Click on the Google Earth icon that you have on your desktop. This is a way to enrich our traveling course by enhancing its appearance. So, these are the steps that you have to follow:

1. Complete the **Fly to** block with the place that you want to pin.

2. Click on the yellow pin, as shown in the following screenshot:

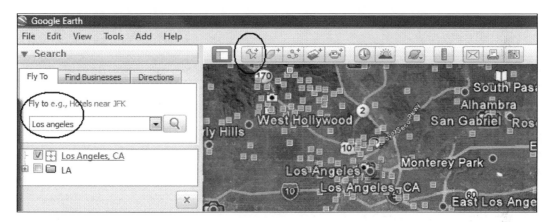

3. A pop-up window will appear. Complete the **Name** block by writing the name of the city.

4. Check the **Latitude** and **Longitude**, so that you place the pin correctly.

5. You may complete the **Description** block.

6. You can change the appearance of the pin by clicking on the pin itself. Another pop-up window will appear showing different sorts of icons, as shown in the following screenshot:

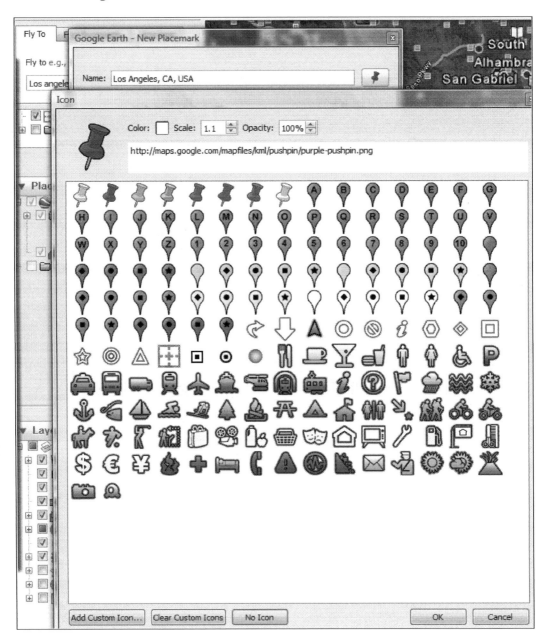

7. You can choose the desired icon by clicking on it | **OK**. The icon that you have selected will appear in the map.

8. Pin as many cities as you are going to work with and repeat steps 1-7.

9. After pinning all the cities, save the file. Click on **File** | **Save** | **Save Place as**.

10. Complete the **File name** block (remember to save the file in the folder which was created for this course) | **Save**.

11. You have already saved the pinned map.

How it works...

We have to insert the map in our Moodle course. In this case, we are going to **Add a resource**, because we are introducing all the activities that are to come. So, choose the weekly outline section where you want to save the resource. These are the steps that you have to follow:

1. Click on **Add a resource** | **File**.

2. Complete the **Name** and **Description** blocks.

3. Click on **Add** | **Browse**.

4. Click on the file that you are going to upload | **Open** | **Upload this file** | **Save and return to course**.

Although we have added a file, students can work with the map interactively!

There's more

We can embed the map in an HTML block in our Moodle course. Click on the downwards arrow next to **Add...** in **Add a block**, as shown in the following screenshot:

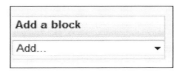

Choose **HTML** and a new block will appear in our Moodle course.

Embedding a map in an HTML block

Open Google Earth and follow these steps in order to embed the map in the block that we have already added:

1. Click on the **View in Google Maps** icon, as shown in the following screenshot:

2. Another window appears. Click on **Link | Customize and preview embedded map**, as shown in the following screenshot:

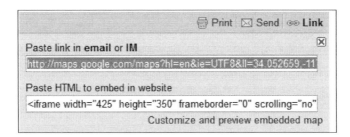

3. Click on **Custom** and adjust the **Width** and **Height**.

4. In the **Preview** section, click on the minus sign and adjust the map to fit the window.

5. Copy the HTML code to embed in our Moodle course.

6. Go back to the Moodle course and click on the configuration icon to embed the map.

7. Complete the **Block title**.

8. In the **Content** block, click on the HTML icon, paste the HTML code which was copied, and click on **Update**.

9. Click on **Save changes**. The map will look as shown in the following screenshot:

Drawing 3D maps using Bing Maps

In this recipe, we will work with the following website: `http://www.bing.com/maps/`. We are going to add social activity to our Moodle course because we are designing a Wiki activity. We ask our students to imagine that they are architects and that they have to travel to San Sebastian, Spain to build a shopping center there. Therefore, we locate the said city in the map using the aforementioned website; you can also use Google Earth, as we did in the other recipes.

Getting ready

We open your default web browser and look for the aforementioned website. We look for San Sebastian, Spain and we select an area in which our students have to locate the shopping center. So, if you do not happen to know the place, there will appear some information on the left-hand side of the margin giving data as well as images of the places that are there.

How to do it...

Follow these steps in order to select an area of the map and embed it to our Moodle course, and also to develop the activity:

1. Click on the star that appears at the bottom on the left-hand margin.

2. Another pop-up window will appear in which you can find several options to carry out. Click on **My Places | New list** in order to save the area of the map. Complete the blocks within the **Properties** section: **Title**, **Notes**, and **Tags** blocks.

3. Click on **Save**.

4. Click on **2D** on the left-hand margin so that you can mark an area within the map.

5. Click on the **Mark an area within the map** icon (circled in the following screenshot) and select the area that you want your students to take into account. Your map will look as shown in the following screenshot:

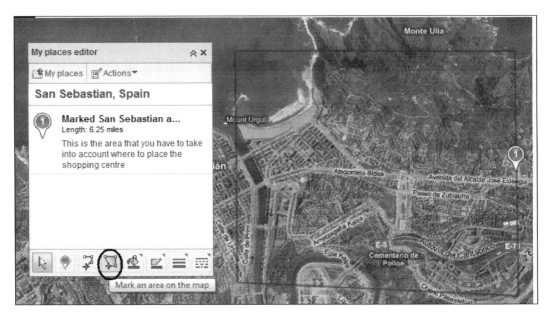

6. Save the changes.

7. Click on the **Share your map** icon, next to the star on the bottom left-hand margin (it looks like an envelope).

8. Click on **Customize and preview**. Embed this part of the map. You can choose to embed either a **Static map** or a **Draggable map**.

9. After you customize your options, click on **Generate code | Copy code** to paste this code in the Moodle course.

How it works...

We have just finished designing the map, the part of the world that we want our students to travel in order to build a shopping center. We enter and choose the weekly outline section where we want to design the activity. We are going to carry out this activity in **Wiki** so that students can interact among themselves:

1. Click on **Add an activity | Wiki**.

2. Complete the **Wiki name** and **Wiki description** blocks.

3. Click on the **HTML** icon and paste the code. Click on **Update**.

4. Click on **Save and return to course**.

5. The activity looks as shown in the following screenshot:

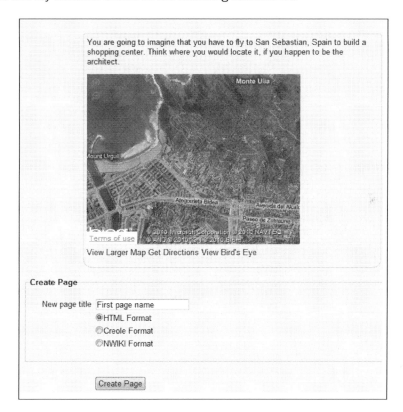

Drawing 3D maps using 3DVIA Shape for Maps

This activity is very appealing because we can draw in a map. We select a city and we can either design a task for our students to draw in the map or we can draw in the map and ask our students for their opinion. In this case, we do the latter. We need a live account in order to publish the model that we create afterwards. Unfortunately, this activity is limited to Windows users.

Getting ready

Open the following website: `http://www.3dvia.com/products/3dvia-shape-for-maps/`. Then click on **Free download**. You can build models such as the one shown in the following screenshot:

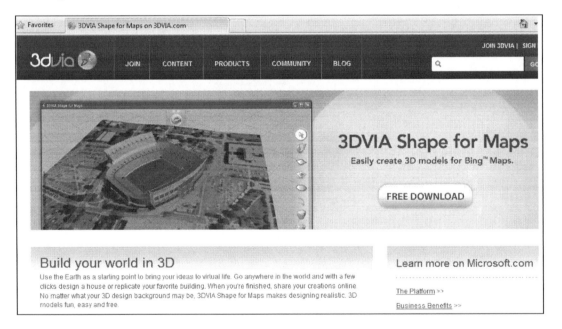

How to do it...

After downloading it, an icon on our desktop will appear. In this activity, we are going to ask our students to travel to Cape Town, South Africa. We design a house and ask them what changes they would make to the house if they happened to go there and live for a school year.

We open 3DVIA Shape for Maps, and the following are the steps that you have to follow in order to design the activity:

1. Type the location that you want to see in the map in the block that says **Type your location here...**, as shown in the following screenshot:

2. Click on the magnifying glass icon. Click on **Road** and bring the map forward.

3. Click on **Start modeling....** The map will appear as a background image. You are going to start modeling your house.

4. Click on the **Grid** icon to check the orientation of the rectangle.

5. Click on the **Rectangle (R)** icon and draw a rectangle; you have to click to start and click to finish, as shown in the following screenshot:

6. Click on the **Push n Pull (P)** icon to add volume to the rectangle. Move the mouse upwards.

7. Click on the **Draw (D)** icon and draw a line in the middle of the roof of the house.

8. Click on the **Deform (M)** icon. Select the line that you have just drawn and drag the yellow arrow in order to create a roof.

9. Click on the **Rectangle (R)** icon again in order to draw the doors and windows of the house.

10. Click on the **Rotate** icon, so that you draw the back doors or windows of the house as well.

11. Click on the **Push n Pull (P)** icon to give volume to the doors and windows.

12. Click on the **Paint (X)** icon, to decorate the house. You can choose different textures, paints, and so on.

13. You can also add some elements to the house such as trees, cars, a swimming pool, and so on. Type what you want to add in the search box at the bottom.

14. Click on **Publish**. Complete the following pop-up window:

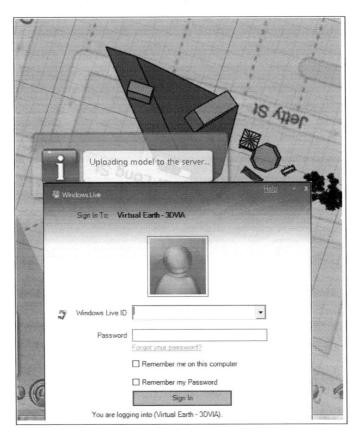

15. Another pop-up window will appear. You have to give a name for the model. Then click on **Publish**.

16. Click on **Display on map**. The house will appear in Bing Maps. It will be as shown in the following screenshot:

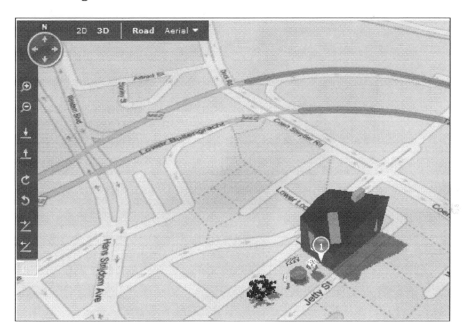

17. In order to embed the map with the image in our Moodle course, see the previous recipe in order to get the embedding code.

How it works...

We have just created the multimedia part of the activity. Now we have to embed it in our Moodle course. We are going to create a **Database** in which we ask our students to give their opinions about the house. Another option would be to create a **Forum** activity where students can debate about this creation. We can work together with the Geography teacher, who can add data about the climate of a said place and add any other changes to the house. These are the steps that you have to follow:

1. Click on **Add an activity | Database**.

2. Complete the **Name** and **Introduction** blocks.

3. Click on the **HTML** icon. Paste the code in order to embed the map. Click on **Update**.

4. Click on **Save and display**.

5. Click on the downwards arrow in **Create a new field** and choose **Text**.

6. Complete the **Field name** with questions. Click on **Add**. Write as many questions as necessary to guide students to think of possible changes to the house, as shown in the following screenshot:

7. Click on **Save | Continue** and go back to the course. The activity is ready to work with!

Using Google maps to locate European bridges

In this recipe, we have the possibility to travel to France, and visit the River Seine. There are a lot of bridges along this river, therefore we ask our students to go along this river by boat. They have to find all the bridges along it and mark them in the map. Another possibility is for us to do this task the other way round and ask them to find some information.

Getting ready

We look for a website giving information about the bridges in the Seine River, such as http://www.pariswater.com/ponts/. In this website, you can find the bridges on the left. As you click on each of them, a bigger picture is displayed in the middle of the page. There is information about the bridge both in English and French. Therefore, we could also work with the French teacher as well as the Geography one!

How to do it...

We work with maps because we have to travel through this beautiful river by boat. Our students will have to locate all the bridges along the Seine River. Therefore, we will work with `http://maps.google.com/`. We visit this website and look for this river. Follow these steps in order to link the map in our Moodle course:

1. After you find the desired location, click on **Link**, as shown in the following screenshot:

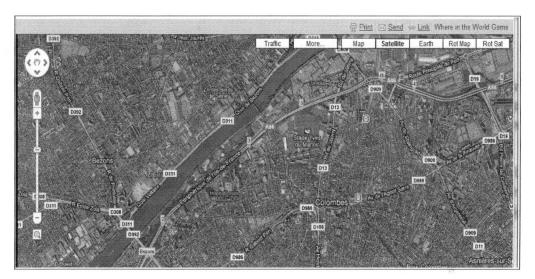

2. Copy the URL because you are going to paste it in the Moodle course.

How it works...

We have the map and the website with the information about the bridges. So, now we can design the activity in **Advanced uploading of files**, in case they need to upload more than one file. Here are the steps that you have to follow:

1. Click on **Add an activity | Advanced uploading of files**.

2. Complete the **Assignment name** and **Description** blocks.

3. Mark a link to the website describing the bridges: `http://www.pariswater.com/ponts/`.

4. Mark a link to the website of the map: `http://goo.gl/maps/2R83`.

5. Click on **Save and return to course**. The activity looks as shown in the following screenshot:

Displaying interactive information about the solar system

The title of the recipe is telling us that we are traveling far away from planet Earth, which means we are no longer traveling by boat or by plane. We have decided to travel as Dennis Tito did on Saturday 28th April, 2001. Yes, we travel in a spaceship and into space. We are going to see the solar system from the window of our rocket.

This is a very simple and appealing recipe because we work with a quite amusing as well as entertaining website. It offers a *free astronomy resource designed to teach children about the exciting world of outer space*, as stated on the website.

Getting ready

Visit the following website: `http://www.kidsastronomy.com/index.htm`. We click on **Solar System**, as shown in the following screenshot:

Image credit: http://www.kidsastronomy.com/index.htm.

How to do it...

We are going to insert a passive activity in our Moodle course; that is to say we add a resource. We choose the weekly outline section where we want to place it. Then, follow these steps in order to carry it out:

1. Click on **Add a resource | URL**.
2. Complete the **Name** and **Description** blocks.

3. Complete the **Content** block and copy the following URL: `http://www.kidsastronomy.com/solar_system.htm`, as shown in the following screenshot:

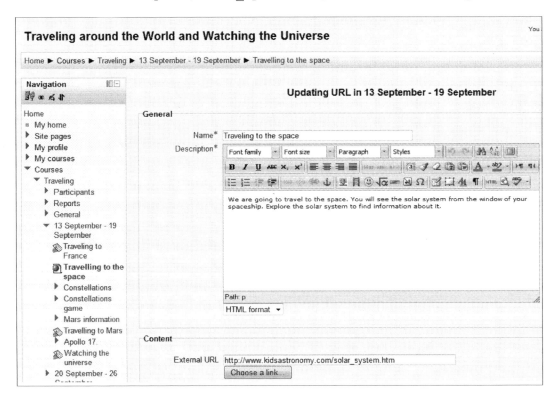

4. Click on **Save and return to course**.

How it works...

As stated before, it is a simple recipe. We can just work with this amazing website. Students click on the planets and information is displayed about them. Thus, you can make any other links or add any other activities, including games. Therefore, the resource looks as shown in the following screenshot:

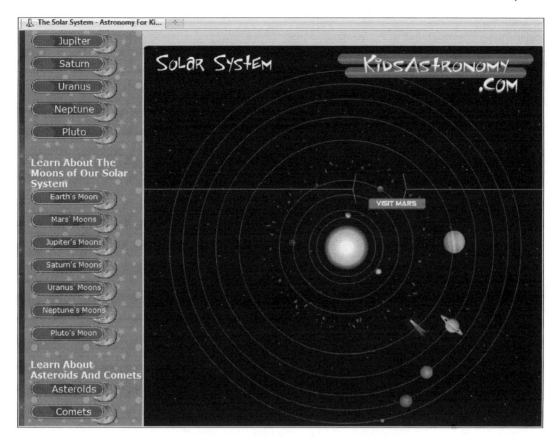

Image credit: `http://www.kidsastronomy.com/solar_system.htm`.

Working with constellation maps

We continue our trip into the space. As you have realized, we started within the Earth and from the previous recipe onwards, we continue in our spaceship. In this recipe, we visit the constellations.

Another accurate trip to work with constellations is to travel back in time and tell our students how sailors used to guide themselves with stars. However, we are not going to use that kind of trip or going back in time; it's just a tip for you to take into account!

Getting ready

We are going to work with space; therefore, we may use Google Earth.

We click on the planet icon and choose **Sky**, as shown circled in the following screenshot:

Another option is to use the following website: `http://www.astroviewer.com/index.php`, which is better because we can embed the map of the constellations. Click on **For your website** and click on **interactive night sky map**. Copy the HTML code so as to embed the map in our Moodle course afterwards.

How to do it...

We have just found what to use to work with constellation maps. It is time to design the activity in our trip. We are traveling, and from the window of our spaceship we can see many stars; as you know, these stars together seen from Earth form different constellations.

We work with this map because students can travel in space and see the constellations in 3D. After they explore the universe, they complete a glossary in our Moodle course with the names of the constellations. They add the necessary information about them. Another option would be to design a **Database** activity instead of a **Glossary**.

Then, they can play a game in which they have to name the constellation. We can add this game as a final task of our project because they already have the necessary information to recognize the constellations in the sky. Thus, we choose the weekly outline section where we want to place the activity and follow these steps in order to carry out the activity in our Moodle course:

1. Click on **Add an activity| Glossary**.
2. Complete the **Name** and **Description** blocks.
3. Click on the **HTML** icon. Paste the HTML code that you have copied from the website in order to embed the sky map of constellations.

4. Click on **Update**.

5. Click on **Save and return to course**. The activity looks as shown in the following screenshot:

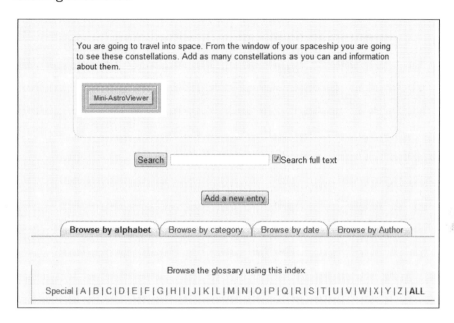

Image credit of the **Mini - AstroViewer** icon embedded in Moodle course: http://www.astroviewer.com. Copyright by Dirk Matussek.

How it works...

After so much work, students deserve to play. Therefore, we make a link to a website in which students can play the constellations game. Follow these steps in order to add the resource:

1. Click on **Add a resource | URL**.

2. Complete the **Name** and **Description** blocks.

3. Complete the **External URL** block within the **Content** box. Copy the following URL: http://www.kidsastronomy.com/astroskymap/constellation_hunt.htm.

4. Click on **Save and return to course**. The activity looks as shown in the following screenshot:

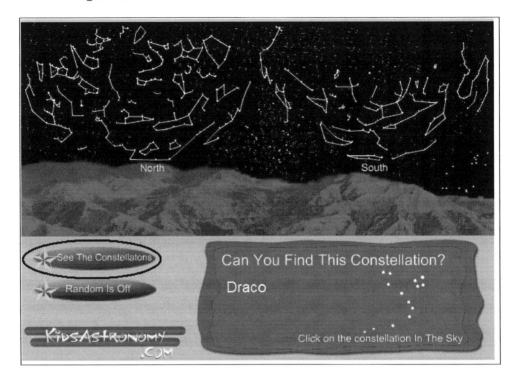

Image credit: `http://www.kidsastronomy.com/astroskymap/constellation_hunt.htm`.

Whenever you click on **See The Constellations**, they are seen with the lines in the sky, as shown in the previous picture.

Embedding a map of Mars

In this recipe, we focus on the Red Planet—Mars. We work with a website that will allow us to embed a map of Mars. Therefore, visit: `http://hubblesite.org/gallery/album/pr1999027f/`. Apart from embedding the map, we also have the possibility of saving the image of the said map so that we can upload it to our Moodle course.

Getting ready

We can also add more information about this planet. Therefore, we can look for data for educators in the following website: `http://tinyurl.com/49agtvy`. According to the type of activity that we are going to develop, we can choose an appropriate link.

Now, it's time to Moodle it!

How to do it...

We design the following activity in two parts. The first part is a resource and the second part consists of the production of our students (the result of the trip). Thus, we ask our students to travel to the Red Planet, but before doing so we have to give them information about the place to visit. Follow these steps in order to add the resource in our Moodle course:

1. Click on **Add a resource | URL**.

2. Complete the **Name** and **Description** blocks.

3. Complete the **External URL** block within the **Content** box. Copy the following URL: `http://tinyurl.com/4lvm2jy`.

4. Click on **Save and return to course**. The activity looks as shown in the following screenshot:

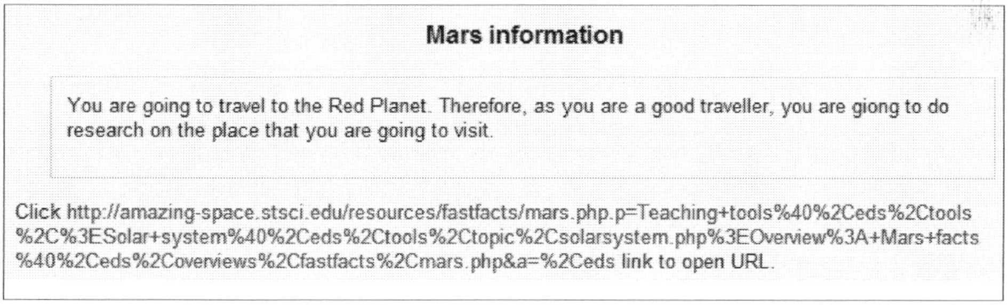

Mars information

You are going to travel to the Red Planet. Therefore, as you are a good traveller, you are giong to do research on the place that you are going to visit.

Click http://amazing-space.stsci.edu/resources/fastfacts/mars.php.p=Teaching+tools%40%2Ceds%2Ctools %2C%3ESolar+system%40%2Ceds%2Ctools%2Ctopic%2Csolarsystem.php%3EOverview%3A+Mars+facts %40%2Ceds%2Coverviews%2Cfastfacts%2Cmars.php&a=%2Ceds link to open URL.

How it works...

We are going to embed the map of Mars because we do not want our students to get lost. After that, we ask them to write down their experience in their virtual journey, including as much information as possible. We can also direct the assignment by guiding them on how to produce their report.

We design the activity in **Upload a single file**. Therefore, follow these steps in order to add the assignment to our Moodle course:

1. Click on **Add an activity |Upload a single file** within **Assignments**.

2. Complete the **Assignment name** and the **Description** blocks.

3. Enter the following website: `http://hubblesite.org/gallery/album/ pr1999027f/`. Click on **EMBED** and copy the HTML code that appears.

4. Go back to the Moodle course, click on **HTML**, and paste the HTML code that you have copied before. Click on **Update**.

5. Click on **Save and return to course**. The activity looks as shown in the following screenshot:

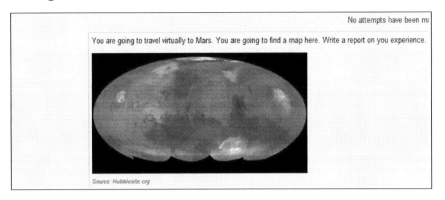

Image credit: `http://hubblesite.org/gallery/album/pr1999027f/`.

Photo credit: Steve Lee (University of Colorado), Jim Bell (Cornell University), Mike Wolff (Space Science Institute), and NASA.

Labeling the moon

In this recipe, we travel to the moon. Therefore, we work with Google Earth again. We label the parts of the moon that we want our students to explore. We can also embed related videos from `http://www.youtube.com`, which are available in Google Earth.

Getting ready

Open Google Earth, click on the planet, and choose **Moon**, as shown in the following screenshot:

How to do it...

We choose a section of the moon that we want our students to explore. We can choose one of the **Apollo Missions** on the left-hand margin in Google Earth within **Layers** in the **Earth Gallery**. We choose **Apollo 17**, because there is also an interesting video available on YouTube that we can embed in order to strengthen our activity. You can search on the said website by just typing "Apollo 17", and several videos appear.

We follow these steps in order to capture a photo labeling the Moon in the part that we want our students to explore. Follow these steps:

1. Click on **Apollo 17**. A pop-up window will appear displaying information about the different resources available.

2. Click on **Zoom in** at the bottom of the window in order to explore the landing site.

3. Click on the **Add placemark** icon on top. Complete the pop-up window, as shown in the following screenshot:

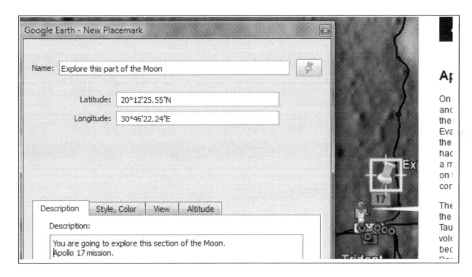

4. Click on **OK**.

5. Click on **File | Save | Save image**.

6. Complete the **File name** block.

7. Click on **Save**.

8. You can also choose a video about this place on the moon to embed it in our Moodle course.

9. Click on **Watch on YouTube**, as shown in the following screenshot:

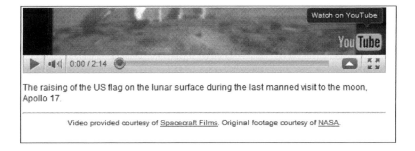

10. Click on **Embed** and copy the HTML code in order to embed the said video in our Moodle course.

How it works...

We have plenty of multimedia assets to work with. It is time to create an activity in our Moodle course about traveling to the moon.

We are going to create a **Forum**, because we want our students to add their opinions about this mission. Therefore, choose the weekly outline section where you want to add the activity and follow these steps:

1. Click on **Add an activity | Forum**.
2. Complete the **Forum name** and the **Forum introduction** blocks.
3. Click on the **Insert / edit image** icon.
4. Click on **Find or upload an image | Upload a file | Browse**.
5. Click on the image of the moon that we had saved before.
6. Click on **Open | Upload this file | Insert**.
7. Complete the **Image description** block.
8. Click on **Insert**.
9. Click on the **HTML** icon.
10. Paste the HTML code from YouTube.
11. Click on **Update**.
12. Click on **Save and return to course**. You have created a rich activity!

Watching the universe

In this recipe, we design a very simple activity. We are going to go on traveling into space and watch the universe. We will explore the other planets. Therefore, let's get ready for our last stop.

Getting ready

We are going to add an offline activity. This time we ask our students to choose a planet to explore. We have already worked with many websites that allow us to work with maps, either to embed them, take a picture of the desired location, or make a link to them. So, you are free to choose.

How to do it...

We are going to choose a website to work with, so that our students are provided with some material to work with. One option is to divide the activity in two parts, adding a resource and afterwards the activity. Another option is to make a link to the website that we are going to work with within the activity. After deciding the website, we design the offline activity. Let's see how it works!

How it works...

We choose the weekly outline section where we want to place our activity. These are the steps that you have to follow:

1. Click on **Add an activity | Offline activity** within **Assignments**.

2. Complete the **Assignment name** and **Description** blocks.

3. Make a link to the website that you are going to work with, if you did not include a resource in the activity.

4. Click on **Save and return to course**. The activity looks as shown in the following screenshot:

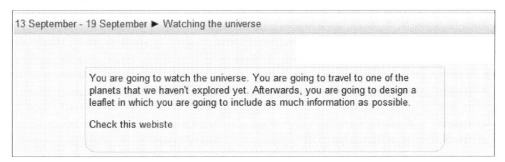

13 September - 19 September ▶ Watching the universe

You are going to watch the universe. You are going to travel to one of the planets that we haven't explored yet. Afterwards, you are going to design a leaflet in which you are going to include as much information as possible.

Check this webiste

See also

▶ *Creating maps with sceneries.*

3
Working with Different Types of Interactive Charts

In this chapter, we will cover:

- ► Inserting column charts
- ► Embedding a line chart
- ► Designing an interactive pie chart with labels
- ► Creating bar charts with hyperlinks
- ► Working with area charts
- ► Inserting an X Y (Scatter) chart
- ► Working with stock charts
- ► Creating a poll and designing a surface chart
- ► Drawing a donut interactive chart
- ► Inserting different types of radar charts

Introduction

This chapter explains how to create and embed 2D and 3D charts. They can also be interactive or static ones and we will insert them in our Moodle courses. Though we are going to work mainly with Open Office Spreadsheet, we will include diverse tools and techniques that are also present. The main idea is to display data in charts and provide students with the necessary information for their activities.

We also work with a variety of charts, and deal with statistics as a baseline topic in this chapter. We can either develop a chart or work with ready-to-use data. We could avoid the math section. However, you could design this in your Moodle course together with a math teacher.

When thinking of statistics, we generally have the picture of a chart in mind and some percentages representing the reading of the said chart. We can change that paradigm and create a different way to draw and read statistics in our Moodle course. We design charts with drawings, links to websites, and other interesting items.

We can also redesign the charts with numbers with different assets because we want to enrich and strengthen the diversity of the material for our Moodle course. Thus, some students are not keen on numbers and dislike activities with them. So, let's give another chance to statistics!

There are different types of graphics to show statistics. Therefore, we show a variety of tools available to display different results. No matter what our subject is, we can include this type of graphics in our Moodle course.

You can use these graphics to help your students give weight to their arguments and express themselves using key points clearly. We teach students, within our subject, to include graphics and read them using them as a tool of communication. Reading charts will broaden their minds.

We can also work with puzzles. That is to say we can invent a graph and give tips or clues to our students so that they can sort out which are the percentages belonging to the chart. In other words, we can create a listening comprehension activity, a reading comprehension one, or a math problem. We just upload or embed the chart, create an appealing activity, and give clues to our students so that they can think of the items belonging to the chart.

Inserting column charts

In this activity, we work with the following website: `http://www.eddataexpress.ed.gov/index.cfm`. We work with statistics about the U.S. government. We will change the format of the chart. We are only going to use the data in order to stick to the figures. We choose a state to work with—New York. We look for the statistics about the population. After reading the content information, we confirm the usage of the data.

Getting ready

Now, we can work with the statistics about New York Students Demographics. There are five percentages in the chart and we take into account those figures in order to design a column chart:

- 0.5 percent of American Indian and Alaskan Native Students: 2008-2009
- 7.7 percent of Asian and Pacific Islander Students: 2008-2009

- ▶ 19.2 percent of Afro-American Students: 2008-2009
- ▶ 21.3 percent of Hispanic Students: 2008-2009
- ▶ 51.0 percent of Anglo-Saxon Students: 2008-2009
- ▶ 0.3 percent Unknown (the data is not available)

How to do it...

We have already found the statistics that we are going to work with. Then, we have to add those figures in a chart. We are going to use **OpenOffice.org**. We can download it from the following website: `http://download.openoffice.org/index.html`.

After installing OpenOffice, we work with **Spreadsheet**. Thus, we click on the said icon. Follow these steps in order to draw the chart:

1. Click on the icon of **Number Format: Percent**, with the % symbol. Then, type the first percentage in **A1**.

2. Enter the demographic information in **B1**.

3. Repeat steps 1 and 2, and then enter the data in **A2**, **B2**, and so on.

4. In **A7**, click on the **Sum** icon. Highlight **A1** up to **A6**; the total percentage will appear there.

5. Highlight **A1** up to **A6** again. Click on **Insert | Chart**, as shown in the following screenshot:

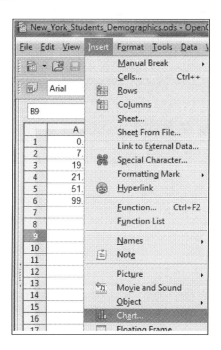

6. Choose **Column**. You can add 3D effects if you click on the **3D Look** block. There are also different types of columns within the **Shape** block, as shown in the following screenshot:

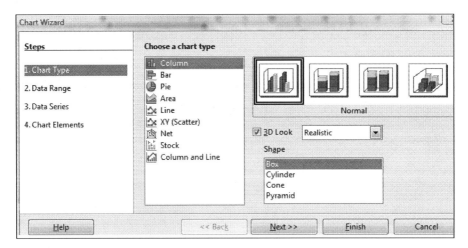

7. Click on **Next** or **Data Range**.

8. The range is the information that you use to display in the chart. You have already highlighted the range; as a result, you have verified that it is correct.

9. Choose whether to show the data in rows or in columns. Click on the radio button **Data series in columns**.

10. Click on **Next** or **Data Series**.

11. Add the information of the percentages. Complete the **Range for Name** block with the absolute directions of the blocks in the spreadsheet. Click on **Add** to add the necessary ones. In this case, we do need six.

12. Click on **Next** or **Chart elements**.

13. Complete the **Title**, **Subtitle**, **X axis**, and **Y axis** blocks with the information about the statistics that you are working with.

14. Click on **Finish**.

15. The chart will appear, as shown in the following screenshot:

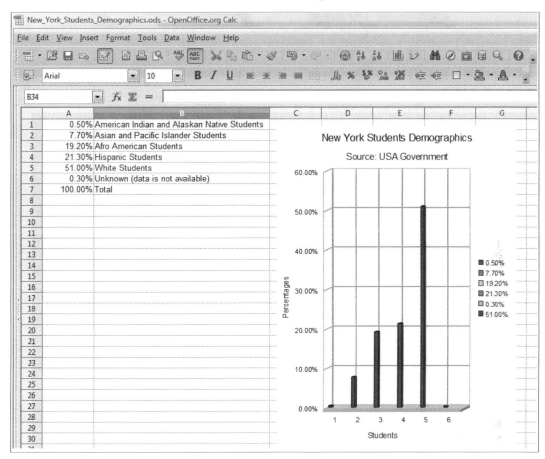

16. You can right-click on the image. Copy it and paste it in software such as Paint or Inkscape and save it as .png. Therefore, you can upload it to the Moodle course as an image.

17. Another possibility is to save the file. Thus, whenever you open it, the chart appears, as shown in the previous screenshot.

How it works...

We have already designed the chart that we are going to work with. It's time to think of an activity. Therefore, an important link to this information is Ellis Island, where many immigrants from different parts of the world arrived. There were many reasons for them to do so, explained in the following website in a timeline: http://www.ellisisland.org/immexp/ wseix_4_3.asp?. We have found a historic connecting element to our chart. We could design the activity in a **Forum**.

We can also upload either the image of the chart or the file that we have created to our activity within the Moodle course. Choose the weekly outline section where you want to insert this activity and follow these steps:

1. Click on **Add an activity | Forum**.

2. Complete the **Forum name** block.

3. Click on the downwards arrow in **Forum type** and choose **Q and A forum**.

4. For uploading the image of the chart, click on the **Insert/edit image** icon | **Find or upload an image** | **Browse**, and look for the image that you have just saved.

5. Click on **Upload this file**.

6. Complete the **Image description** block and click on **Insert**.

7. Make a link to the aforementioned website.

8. Click on **Save and return to course**. The activity looks as shown in the following screenshot:

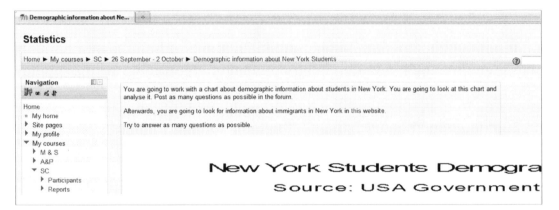

Embedding a line chart

In this recipe, we will present the estimated number of people (in millions) using a particular language over the Internet. To do this, we will include images in our line chart. Instead of writing the name of the languages, we will insert the flags, which will represent the language used. It is the first asset that we have inserted in our statistics drawings in order to make them more appealing to the sight of our students. We design the line chart, taking into account the statistics carried out in the following website: http://www.internetworldstats.com/stats7.htm.

Getting ready

We have an element (the image) that we are going to use in this recipe though we have to decide what to use in order to develop the line chart. We are going to carry out the activity using the following website `https://documents.google.com/?hl=en#all`. We have to sign in and follow the steps required in order to design a spreadsheet file. We have several options to work with the document. After you have an account to work with Google Docs, let's see how to do our line chart!

How to do it...

We work with Spreadsheet because we need to make calculations and create a chart. Therefore, we need to follow these steps:

1. Click on **File | New | Spreadsheet**.
2. Write the name of the languages spoken in column **A**.
3. Write the figures in column **B**.
4. Select the figures from column **B1** up to **B11**. Click on **Insert | Chart**.
5. Complete the options, as shown in the following screenshot:

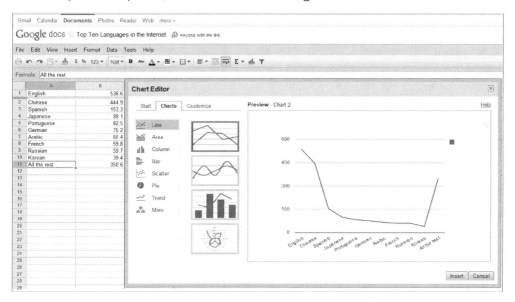

6. Click on **Save chart**.
7. Add the images of the flags belonging to the languages spoken. Then click on **Insert | Image...**.
8. Another pop-up window will appear. You may either copy the **URL link** in the block or use the **Google image search**.

9. There are many warnings about copyright issues. You should look for one flag for each language and place it next to the chart that we have already designed in our document. Check that the image is free to use without copyright.

10. Click on the downwards arrow in **Share | Publish as a web page**, as shown in the following screenshot:

11. Another pop-up window appears. Click on the downwards arrow below **Get a link to the published data**, as shown in the following screenshot:

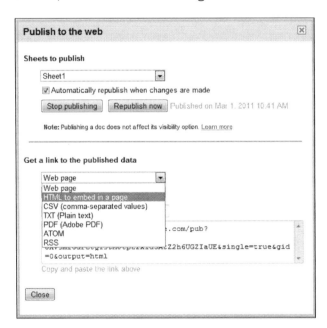

12. Click on **HTML to embed in a page**, as shown in the previous screenshot.

13. Copy the HTML code that appears in the block that reads **Copy and paste the link above**.

14. Click on **Close**.

How it works...

We have just designed the chart that we want our students to work with. We are going to embed the chart with the flags. If you want to design a warm up activity for students to guess or find out which are the top languages used in the Internet; you could add a chat or a forum in the course. After that, we design the activity making a link to the interactive chart in a **Wiki**.

Select the weekly outline section where you want to add the activity and follow these steps:

1. Click on **Add an activity | Wiki**.

2. Complete the **Wiki name** and **Wiki description** blocks.

3. Click on the **HTML** icon and paste the HTML code that we have previously copied. Then click on **Update**.

4. Click on **Save and return to course**. The activity looks as shown in the following screenshot:

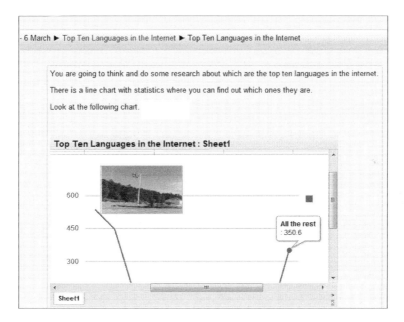

When hovering the mouse on the line chart, apart from looking at the flags, students can read the name of the language and the exact percentage of the statistic due to the fact that the chart is interactive, as shown in the previous screenshot.

See also

► *Designing an interactive pie chart with labels*

Designing an interactive pie chart with labels

In this recipe, we work with an interactive chart, which is to be created after conducting a survey on our students. Therefore, our first step is to design a survey in our Moodle course.

How to do it...

We design an activity to ask our students to vote in order to create the interactive pie chart. We create the activity in a choice so that students can choose their favorite type of computer games. Afterwards, we draw the interactive chart with the results.

Choose the weekly outline section where you want to add the activity. These are the steps that you are going to follow:

1. Click on **Add an activity | Choice**.

2. Complete the **Choice name** and **Introduction text** blocks.

3. Complete the **Options** blocks.

4. Complete the **Restrict answering to this time period**, **Miscellaneous Settings**, and **Common module settings** blocks, as shown in the following screenshot:

5. Click on **Save and return to course**.

How it works...

Students click on the activity and vote. The way that this activity was designed, it won't allow students to vote more than once. This activity works as shown in the following screenshot:

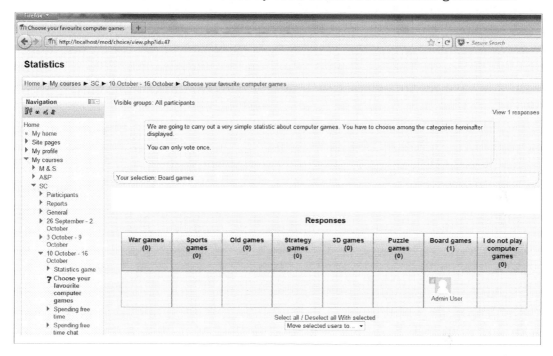

By the way, I have voted for board games; as you can see, I have no choice to vote again, and also we can see how many people voted.

There's more

After gathering the votes of our students, we can design the pie chart showing the results. Therefore, we can use Google Docs to create the interactive chart, write the data, and insert the chart, as shown in the following screenshot:

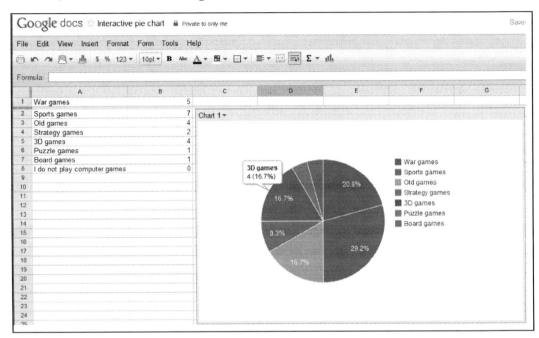

We have just used Google Docs like in the previous recipe, so we follow the same steps in order to create the chart, but in this case we choose pie chart.

Inserting an interactive pie chart with labels

We have already designed the chart in Google Docs and it is time to upload it in our Moodle course. We can create several types of activities where we can use the pie chart as a resource to enhance our Moodle course. The only step that we have to bear in mind is to copy the HTML code as we did in the previous recipe in order to paste it and embed the chart in our Moodle course.

In order to get the HTML code from Google Docs, follow these steps:

1. Click on the downwards arrow in **Share | Publish as a web page**.

2. Another pop-up window appears. Click on the downwards arrow below **Get a link to the published data**.

3. Click on **HTML to embed in a page**.

4. Copy the HTML code that appears in the block that reads **Copy and paste the link above**.

5. Click on **Close**.

6. Now that we have the HTML code, we can paste it in any activity that we want to design in our Moodle course.

See also

▸ *Embedding a line chart*

Creating bar charts with hyperlinks

In this recipe, we are going to perform a very simple activity. We are going to use Open Office Spreadsheet, which we have already used before. Another option happens to be Microsoft Excel. You can download a free trial version from the following website: `http://tinyurl.com/27xe849`.

Getting ready

We design a **Database** activity in our Moodle course to survey students according to the way they spend their free time. We just carry out a simple statistic; we are not focusing on other factors, though a Math teacher can help us. We design this activity in two parts so that the first part is the survey to our students and the second part consists of gathering the data and designing a chart using Open Office Spreadsheet, creating the hyperlinks through a website, and uploading it to our Moodle course.

How to do it...

We are going to enter our Moodle course and design the database activity in order to gather information about the way our students spend their free time. Select the weekly outline section and follow these steps in order to develop the activity:

1. Click on **Add an activity | Database**.

2. Complete the **Name** and the **Introduction** fields.

3. Choose **1** in **Maximum entries**.

4. Click on **Save and display**.

5. Click on the downwards arrow in **Create a new field** and choose **Radio buttons**, as shown in the following screenshot:

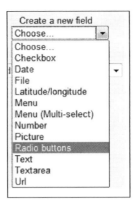

6. Complete at least three **Radio buttons** with free time activities that our students may perform.

7. Click on **Add**.

8. Repeat steps 5-7 at least twice. Complete the **Radio buttons field** with "Spending your free time at weekends" and "Spending your free time on holidays". You may decide to add any other option.

9. Go back to the course. The activity looks as shown in the following screenshot:

How it works...

We have just designed the survey to carry out in our class. Now, it is time to design the bar chart to insert in our Moodle course telling the rest of the class how their friends spend their free time on the different occasions. We are going to work with Open Office Spreadsheet. Follow these steps so that you can design the activity:

1. Complete the spreadsheet with the information that you obtain from the database activity from the Moodle course.

2. Select the first group of columns with the figures, click on **Insert | Chart**, and choose a graph.

3. The chart will appear. You may edit the chart as you wish.

4. Save the file. The file looks as shown in the following screenshot:

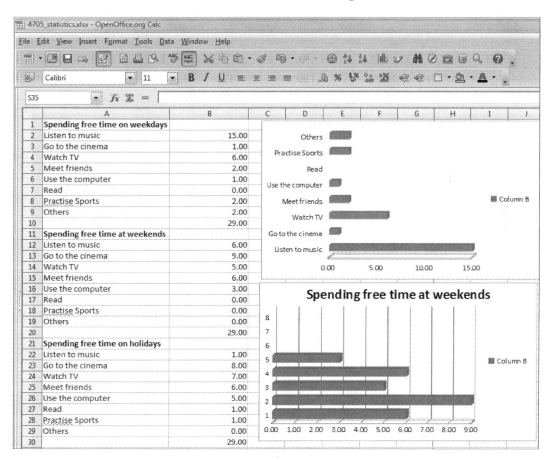

There's more

We can insert hyperlinks in the chart that we have just created using a website because it is not possible to do it in Open Office Spreadsheet. Therefore, we are going to save the charts as images. There are several ways to do this. The simplest way is to press the *Print Screen* key and paste the image in Paint or Inkscape. Cut and paste the chart where you want to add the hyperlinks and save it as `.png`. Repeat the same process for the other two charts.

Inserting hyperlinks to the images

We have just saved the charts as images. Therefore, we can add hyperlinks to those images. It is very simple. We can do it through a web page: `http://www.image-maps.com/`. Follow these steps in order to get the hyperlinks:

1. Click on **Browse** | choose the image that you want to upload | **Open**.

2. Click on **Start Mapping Your Image**, as shown in the following screenshot:

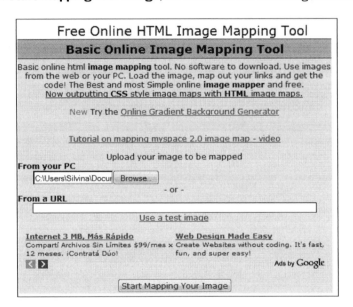

3. Click on **continue to next step**.

4. Click on **Rectangle** | Drag-and-drop the rectangle that appears and forms the shape to cover the bar of the chart.

5. Complete the **Link for this map** and **Title/Alt for this map** blocks.

6. Click on **Save**.

7. Repeat steps 4-6 for each bar. When you finish adding the hyperlinks, click on **Get your code**.

8. Click on **HTML Code**. You will get the code to embed in our Moodle course. Search for the name of the file that you have uploaded and erase the website information; just leave the name of the file. You have to upload the image with the same name so as to have the same file in the Moodle course and in the code. It is shown in the following screenshot:

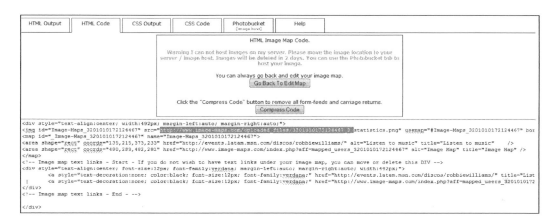

9. Copy the code.

Enter the Moodle course. Create an activity for students to discuss their different likes and dislikes of their ways of spending their free time. First, upload the image to the Moodle course. Create the activity and paste the code that will display the chart with the hyperlinks. The following is an example of a chat activity. When hovering the mouse on the bar, a hyperlink is displayed:

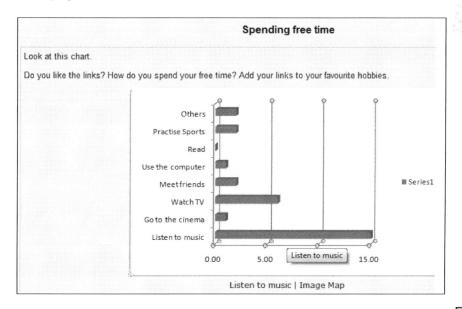

Working with area charts

We are going to design this activity using the following website: `http://sheet.zoho.com/login.do?serviceurl=/home.do`. First of all, you have to **Sign Up for Free** and then we can design our chart there. It is very interesting because we can embed the chart in our Moodle course.

Getting ready

We are not going to survey our students. We can look for online statistics about any topic, or we can upload an existing file to the aforementioned website. Therefore, we use the previous activity that we designed in Open Office and upload it to `sheet.zoho.com`.

How to do it...

You have to follow these steps in order to design the activity:

1. Click on **Import | Browse** | Click on the file that you want to upload | **Open | Import**, as shown in the following screenshot:

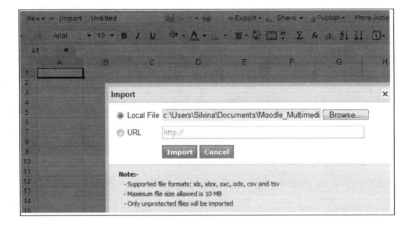

2. Click on **Import**. The file created in Open Office will appear in this website. Create an area chart.

3. Select the information in order to create the chart. Click on **Add chart**.

4. Click on **Area chart**. Select the sub type and click on **Next**.

5. Complete the **Source Data** block, then click on **Next**.

6. Complete the **Options** block, then click on **Done**.

7. Click on the chart. Click on **Publish**, as shown in the following screenshot:

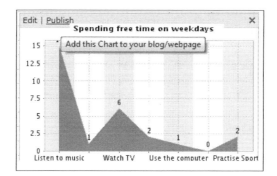

8. A pop-up window displaying the HTML code will appear. Click on **Select Snipped**, and right-click and copy the code so that we can embed the chart in our Moodle course, as shown in the following screenshot:

9. Click on **Close**.
10. Save the file in this: `sheet.zoho.com`.

How it works...

We did not create a chart in this activity because the idea was that you learned how to use an existing one and import it to another online spreadsheet. It is time to embed this area chart to our Moodle course. Therefore, we add a third element to the activity that we have first designed as a database. We are going to create a **Chat** activity so that there is interaction among our students and they can talk about their activities in their free time. Follow these steps:

1. Click on **Add an activity | Chat**.
2. Complete the **Name of this chat room** and **Introduction text** fields.

3. Click on the **HTML** icon and copy the HTML code of the chart. You may embed the three charts that we have designed. In this case, you have to go back to `sheet.zoho.com` and copy the different HTML code for the other charts.

4. Click on **Save and display**. The activity looks as shown in the following screenshot:

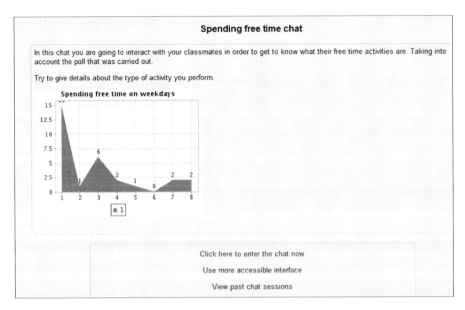

Inserting an X Y (Scatter) chart

This is a very simple recipe. We design and insert an X Y (Scatter) chart in our Moodle course using `http://www.editgrid.com/`.

Getting ready

We ask our students through a **Choice**, as we have done in a previous recipe, if they have traveled abroad on holidays. This is a suggestion; you may change the subject of the poll. As it is a yes/no poll, it is very easy to design a chart. Let's see how to do it!

How to do it...

We enter our Moodle course and select the weekly outline section. We just design a poll in order to gather data to insert the chart afterwards. Therefore, we limit the choice to one week. These are the steps that we have to follow:

1. Click on **Add an activity | Choice**.
2. Complete the **Choice name** and **Introduction text** blocks.

3. Write **YES** in the **Option 1** block and **NO** in the **Option 2** block.

4. Tick the block **Restrict answering to this time period** and choose the **Open** and **Until** date that you are going to poll your students.

5. Within the **Miscellaneous Settings** blocks, click on the downwards arrow in **Allow choice to be updated** and choose **No**, so that students cannot change their choice.

6. Click on **Save and return to course**, the choice looks as shown in the following screenshot:

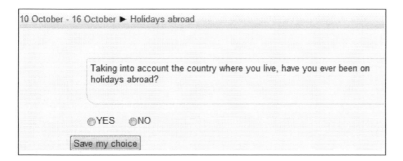

How it works...

After polling our students, we design the chart and insert it in our Moodle course in order to design another activity. We enter `http://www.editgrid.com/workspace`. These are the steps that you have to follow:

1. Click on **New**. Click on **File** | **Save** | Write a name to the file | Within the **Access level**, choose **Public Read – only**.

2. Complete the spreadsheet in order to design a chart afterwards. Select the fields you want to design the chart. Click on the **Insert Chart** icon.

3. Choose **XY Scatter** and choose the one type you want to work with. Click on **Insert**.

4. The chart is shown on the spreadsheet. If you right-click on the chart you can edit it and have the **Object's Permalink** where you can have access to the chart making a link to a website, as shown in the following screenshot:

5. You can also embed the chart in the Moodle course. Click on **Publish | Widgets | HTML Table**, as shown in the following screenshot:

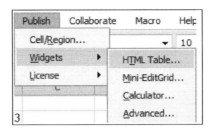

6. A pop-up window will appear with the HTML code to copy and paste in our Moodle course.

You can create a **Forum** activity, embedding the chart in which students post their comments about their holidays abroad.

Working with stock charts

We are going to work with very interesting websites that will brighten our Moodle course. As we deal with stock charts, it is a must that we surf on the NYSE website. There happens to be a useful poster in Adobe Acrobat PDF format that can be added as a resource to our Moodle course, explaining how to read a stock chart. Then, we make a link to another website, where we can create a portfolio online, and when hovering the mouse over the name of the company, we have the stock charts of the company.

Getting ready

We enter http://www.nyse.com/. On the left-hand margin, there is a cascade menu where you can have access to a poster that reads: "Poster: How to Read Stock Tables". Click on **About us | Education | Education Materials**. There will appear new information on the right-hand margin displaying many resources concerning the stock market. We are going to use the aforementioned under **Publications For Teachers**.

Click on it and copy the URL: http://www.nyse.com/pdfs/NYSE_posterA_Mech.pdf .

How to do it...

We enter our Moodle course and choose the weekly outline section. In this case, it is a passive one, giving information about the terms related to stock tables. Follow these steps:

1. Click on **Add a resource | URL**.
2. Complete the **Name** field.
3. Complete the **Description** field.

4. Complete the **Content** field and copy the following URL: `http://www.nyse.com/pdfs/NYSE_posterA_Mech.pdf`.

5. Click on **Save and return to course**.

How it works...

We are going to create a **Forum** activity, because finance is a nice topic to discuss. We work with different links to websites that enrich the forum. You can ask the Accounts department at school for help, if you do not happen to be a finance lover, in order to interact with the said subject.

Remember to add the activity after the previous resource. These are the steps that you have to follow:

1. Click on **Add an activity | Forum**.

2. Complete the **Forum name** and **Forum introduction** blocks.

3. Click on the **Insert / edit image** icon, and minimize the website because you do not need to use it now.

4. Open your default web browser and open it in the following website: `http://finviz.com/`.

5. Click on **Maps** on the top menu, as shown in the following screenshot:

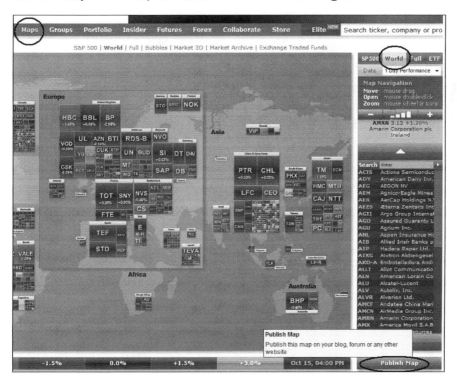

6. Click on **World** on the right-hand side menu at the top. There will appear a map of the world displaying the names of the companies belonging to the countries with stocks. You have access to financial information about them, as shown in the previous screenshot.

7. Click on **Publish Map** at the bottom of the right-hand of the screen, as shown in the previous screenshot. There will appear a pop-out window displaying two URLs, either for a **Large map** or a **Small map**. It's a .PNG URL so copy it and paste it in the **Insert/edit image** block in our Moodle course, which we had minimized before.

8. Complete the **Image description** block and click on **Insert**. Minimize the Moodle course again and go back to http://finviz.com/.

9. Click on **Portfolio** on the top menu.

10. In the **Ticker** block, write the names of some companies, the acronyms used in the map that you have just inserted in our Moodle course.

11. Repeat the same process, and when you finish, write a name to the portfolio in the **Portfolio Name** block. Click on **Save Changes**.

12. Click on **View**. The portfolio looks as shown in the following screenshot:

13. When hovering the mouse on the name of a company, a stock chart is displayed. Copy the URL so that you make a link to this portfolio that was just created. Go back to our Moodle course.

14. Click on the **Insert/edit link** icon and complete the block. Paste the URL that you have just copied.

15. Click on **Update**.

16. Click on **Save and return to course**. The activity looks as shown in the following screenshot:

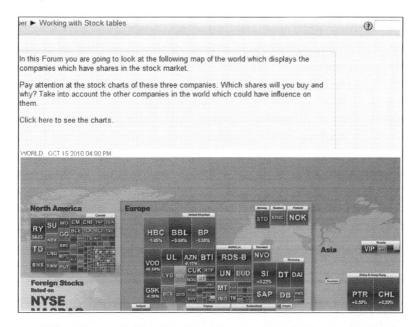

Creating a poll and designing a surface chart

We are going to create another poll in our Moodle course. In previous recipes, we have already done a poll, but this time we design it through **Feedback**. We ask the students and they have to provide their answers. Let's get ready!

Getting ready

We design the poll using Feedback within activities, and we create the chart drawing by exporting the file from Moodle. Feedback has this advantage. The poll is related to Music. The question is: Which device do you use to listen to music?

How to do it...

We enter our Moodle course and choose the weekly outline section where we want to place the activity and follow these steps in order to carry out the activity:

1. Click on **Add an activity | Feedback**.

2. Complete the **Name** and **Description** blocks.

3. Click on **Save and display**.

4. Click on **Edit questions** on the top menu. Click on the downwards arrow within the **Add question to activity** block and select **Short text answer**, as shown in the following screenshot:

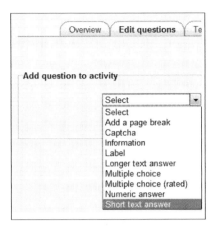

5. Write the question: "Which device do you use to listen to music?" in the **Question** block.

6. Click on **Save question**.

7. Go back to the course.

How it works...

Students will answer the poll only once. We can see the answers of the poll and we can export the files to Open Office or Microsoft Excel, and we can draw a chart using them without typing the data. Feedback generates an .xls file. The said file can be opened with either Microsoft Excel or Open Office spreadsheet, it all depends which one is used on your computer. Follow these steps in order to draw the surface chart:

1. Click on **Analysis | Export to Excel** (or Open Office is also possible depending on which software you use).

2. A pop-up window will appear displaying a message to open the file. Click on **OK**.

3. Save the file. Divide the listeners of music between boys and girls because you need two elements to take into account when drawing a surface chart.

4. Highlight the necessary data to draw a surface chart. Click on **Insert | Other Charts | Surface** (you may also use another type of chart such as bars).

5. The chart may look as shown in the following screenshot:

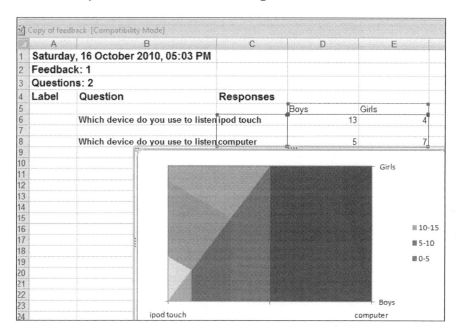

6. Right-click on the chart and select copy. Paste the chart in Paint or Inkscape and save the file as .PNG. In that case, you can upload the image of the chart in the Moodle course and design another activity showing the students the result of the poll.

It is also possible to do it in Open Office spreadsheet if that happens to be software that you use.

Drawing a donut interactive chart

We are going to create an interactive chart with Open Office Drawing. We can insert a chart in a very simple way. We also add images to the chart and hyperlinks to the images. We can also design the same type of activity saving the image as .PNG and use http://www.image-maps.com/.

Getting ready

We are going to work with statistics of the nationality of our students in the school. We first enter the continents' nationalities. If you happen to live in a cosmopolitan city, it would be very interesting! We then add hyperlinks to websites displaying information about the continents.

How to do it...

Enter Open Office **Drawing** and follow these steps to carry out the activity:

1. Click on **Insert | Chart**.

2. Right-click on the chart and choose **Chart Data Table**.

3. Complete the table with the information to display on the chart, using the nationality of the students in the classroom or the school.

4. Right-click again on the chart and choose **Chart Type**.

5. Choose **Pie | Exploded Donut Chart**.

6. Tick **3D Look**.

7. Click on **OK**.

8. Click on **Insert | Picture | From file**.

9. Insert one image related to each continent for each piece of the chart.

10. Click on the image | **Hyperlink**. Complete the block with the hyperlinks. The file will look as shown in the following screenshot:

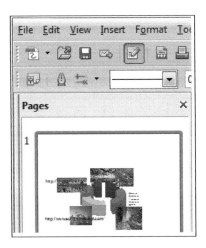

How it works...

We have just designed a chart with hyperlinks with Open Office. We can insert it in our Moodle course as a resource. So, we can design an activity in several parts. You can make a survey to know the nationality of students if you do not happen to have this kind of information (as we have done in previous recipes). Then, create the chart in **Drawing** within Open Office (that is your homework!), and add the file as a resource in the Moodle course. Finally, create an Online text activity within **Assignments**, asking students which continent they find appealing to visit and why based on the information.

4
Integrating Interactive Documents

In this chapter, we will cover:

- ▶ Developing collaborative writing exercises with Google Docs
- ▶ Using Open Office and uploading the file to Moodle
- ▶ Using Flickr images in Open Office documents
- ▶ Including live PDF documents in Moodle exercises
- ▶ Reviewing PDF documents
- ▶ Designing a Wiki

Introduction

This chapter explains how to use diverse types of interactive documents in Moodle courses. The recipes use the most popular, free, web-based, commercial, and desktop-based software to create the interactive documents and provide students the necessary information for their research activities.

Integrating interactive documents in our Moodle courses is a very important asset to take into account. Students not only have the possibility to work with another tool to edit their works, but also use different types of elements that each of them own as a characteristic. Each of the following software that we will look at in the upcoming recipes is eligible according to the type of activity that will be carried out.

The baseline topic of this chapter will be *Fact or Fiction*. There are plenty of activities that can be carried out using this baseline topic. According to the subject that you are teaching, you can change the activities in such a way so that you can adapt the content of the recipe to design a multimedia activity in your Moodle courses.

One of the new features of Moodle 2.0 is that it allows uploading files directly from the file picker from the different places from where we have created them; therefore, as we are dealing with interactive documents in this chapter, we cover how to do it. We do need to have access to manage the repositories in order to achieve this. Thus, we will learn how to do it.

Depending on the subject that you are teaching or the type of activity that you want to design, you can combine these recipes with integrating interactive documents with any of the recipes in *Chapter 3, Working with Different Types of Interactive Charts*. As most of the recipes in this chapter use the same software, thus you can apply the tips and tricks you learnt in the previous chapter.

Recipes are not only based on the different tools that software have, but also on the several ways that students can take advantage of them. In other words, collaborative writing is also possible using those tools. These specific characteristics are to be pointed out in each of the recipes.

Moodle per se allows us to carry out activities in collaborative writing, but the focus is on multimedia assets, that is the reason why we deal with them. Besides, students will be learning that there are plenty of options and many tools that can also be applied for integrating interactive documents.

Developing collaborative writing exercises with Google Docs

In this recipe, we will deal with Google Docs because we want students to write in a collaborative way. There are plenty of options that can be carried out according to the type of activity that needs to be designed; that is to say, the way it can be uploaded into our Moodle course.

Getting ready

First of all, enter the following website: `https://docs.google.com/`. If you have already used this online software, you must have an account; otherwise, you have to sign in so as to create a document. Therefore, enter the previous website, sign in, and choose **Documents**.

How to do it...

The Yeti is the topic to be covered in this recipe because *Fact or Fiction* is the baseline topic that is to be covered in this chapter. Now, we can create the activity—the first part of the activity—in this document. Thus, the following are the steps that you have to follow:

1. Create a file that is to start a debate among students whether the Yeti is a fact or fiction. You can make a link to a website that gives information about the creature, as shown in the following screenshot:

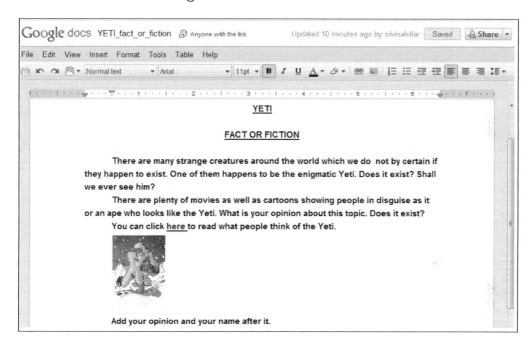

2. Click on **File | Save |** write a name for the file and save it.

3. Click on **Share** on the top right-hand margin. Choose **Anyone who has the link can view**, as shown in the following screenshot:

4. Click on **Close**.

How it works...

We have just created the file that students can modify in a collaborative way. It is time to upload it to our Moodle course. Choose the weekly outline section where you want to insert this activity and follow these steps:

1. Click on **Add an activity | Online text**.

2. Complete the **Assignment name** and the **Description** blocks.

3. Click on **Insert / edit link** icon. Make a link to the website of Google Docs, shown in the previous screenshot.

4. Click on **Save and return to course**. The activity looks as shown in the following screenshot:

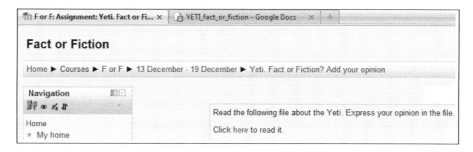

There's more...

You could also incorporate the following other options in your Moodle course:

Uploading a file from Google Docs from Moodle's file picker

One of the new features of Moodle 2.0 is that you can upload files from different sources. You can open the files that you have created directly from Moodle's file picker. So, as the file has been created in Google Docs, we can have access to it from the file picker in Moodle.

Enabling Google Docs in Moodle

There are some steps that you have to take into account in order to enable the Google Docs options in the file picker. First of all, you have to switch role to "manager" in order to have access to the options that we need to work with. After switching role, these are the steps that we have to follow:

1. Click on **Site administration | Plugins | Repositories | Manage repositories**.

2. Click on **Enabled and visible** for **Google Docs**, as shown in the following screenshot:

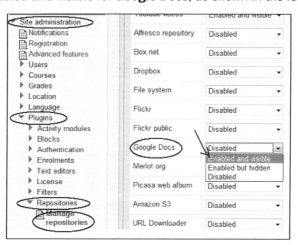

3. Click on **Save | Save changes**.

Uploading a file from Google Docs into Moodle

We can add a resource in our Moodle course by uploading files from Google Docs directly from the file picker because it's just been enabled. So, let's add a resource. Choose the weekly outline section where you want to add the resource and follow these steps:

1. Click on **Add a resource | File**.
2. Complete the **Name** and **Description** blocks.
3. Click on **Add…**, the pop-up window with the **File picker** will appear, as shown in the following screenshot:

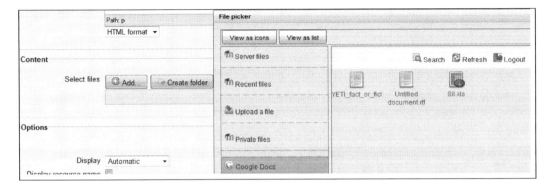

4. Click on **Google Docs**, as shown in the previous screenshot.
5. Choose the file that you want to upload | **Select this file**.
6. Click on **Save and return to course**.

In the previous activity, we have added a resource in Moodle, that is to say we have just uploaded a file for our students to read, therefore, students cannot modify the file. How to enable Google Docs in Moodle 2.0 is a new feature.

See also

In *Chapter 3, Working with Different Types of Interactive Charts*, see:

▶ *Embedding a line chart*

▶ *Designing an interactive pie chart with labels*

Using Open Office and uploading the file to Moodle

Open Office has already been used in the previous chapter in order to draw a chart, but in this chapter, we are using it to write some text. Our students have this software, otherwise they can download it for free; one important reason why we are dealing with it.

Getting ready

We will design an activity in which students give their opinions if some things that happen are fact or fiction. Therefore, we can develop the task in two parts: a resource and an activity.

How to do it...

First of all, we need to design the resource because we have to create a new file in Open Office. In said file, we make a link to a website in which students can have access to more information about the topic to be covered. In this case, we give more data about the strange creature—the Yeti, and add Bigfoot, also known as Sasquatch. Click on **Open Office | Documents** and follow these steps:

1. Create a new file.

2. Make a link to a website that gives information about the two creatures, as shown in the following screenshot:

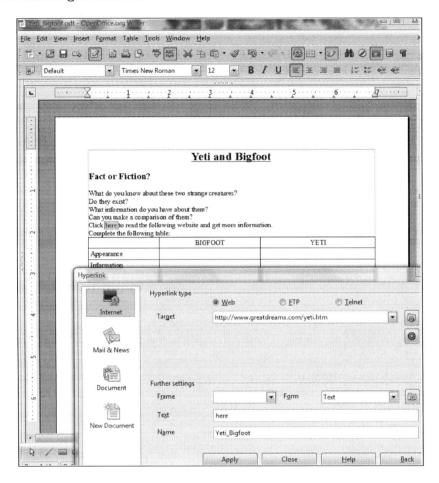

3. Click on **Apply**.

4. Click on **File | Save as |** write a name for the file.

How it works...

After designing the resource, we create within assignments another activity in which students upload a file. That is to say, student have to complete the table that we have created, uploading it to the Moodle course.

Choose the weekly outline section where you want to add the resource. These are the steps to follow:

1. Click on **Add a resource | File**.

2. Complete the **Name** and **Description** blocks.

3. Click on **Add | Upload a file | Browse** | look for the file that has been created and click on it | **Open | Upload this file**.

4. Click on **Save and return to course**.

5. The resource is ready! It looks as shown in the following screenshot:

6. Let's create the activity. Click on **Add an activity | Upload a single file** within **Assignments**.

7. Complete the **Assignment name** and the **Description** blocks. Point out that students have to fill in the previous file and submit it.

8. Click on **Save and return to course**.

We combined the resource with the activity. Open Office does not allow us to use a file in a collaborative way like Google Docs, but we can adjust this using the resource and activity that Moodle offers.

Using Flickr images in Open Office documents

In the previous recipe, the same software was used; therefore, we can modify the previous file and add images of those creatures from Flickr. We work with external files because Open Office does not have a clipart library. Thus, this tool is the right option.

Getting ready

We can both search for a photo in Flickr or upload a picture from our personal collection. However, I doubt that we have a photo of these creatures! Therefore, visit `http://www.flickr.com/`, and create a free account, and upload photos to our document in Open Office.

How to do it...

After signing in and creating the account, search for photos that people have uploaded. Therefore, these are the steps to follow in order to find photos to insert in our Open Office file:

1. Click on the downwards arrow in the **Search** block on the left and choose **Everyone's Uploads**.

2. In the **Search** block on the right, write **yeti**, because we need photos of the said creature, as shown in the following screenshot:

3. Click on **Search** and on the image that you want to insert in the file.

4. Right-click on the image and choose **Save Picture As**. Bear in mind to select a free license image.

5. Another option is to right-click on the image and click on **Copy**. Then you go to the document and paste the image.

How it works...

We have just selected the images that need to be uploaded in our document. They can be uploaded in two ways, though it would be better to save the image in case we need it another time. So, these are the steps to follow:

1. Open the previous document in Open Office.

2. Click on **Insert** | **Picture** | **From file...** | select the image to upload | **Open**.

3. Enlarge the image so that it fits the table designed.

4. Another option is to right-click on the place where the image is to be pasted and click on **Paste**.

5. Save the file. The file looks as shown in the following screenshot:

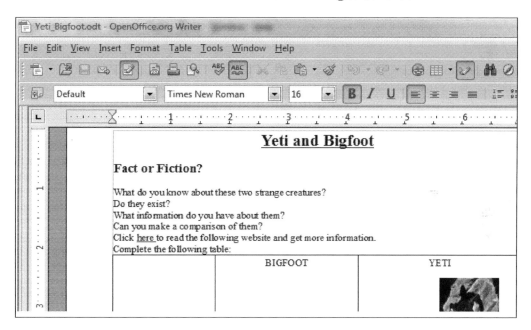

See also

▸ *Using Open Office and uploading the file to Moodle.*

Including live PDF documents in Moodle exercises

This recipe is very interesting and appealing for our students. We can develop any type of activities using this resource, because we are inserting Adobe Reader within our Moodle course. For that reason, we do need to work with some code. Let's get ready!

Getting ready

Open Office is needed in order to convert a file that we have just designed into a PDF. Use the same file to avoid creating a new one. Besides, you may use one of the activities that you have saved in your computer and convert it to carry out this activity.

Another software needed for this recipe is Adobe Reader, which can be downloaded from the following website: `http://get.adobe.com/reader/download/`.

How to do it...

First of all, convert the file into a PDF. Therefore, choose the file used in the previous recipe and follow these steps to convert it:

1. Enter **Open Office | Text Document**.

2. Click on **Open |** and browse for the file to be converted into a PDF.

3. Click on **File | Export as PDF | Export**, as shown in the following screenshots:

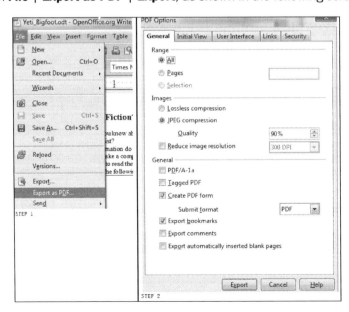

4. Write a name for the file. Click on **Save**.

5. You can now open the file using Adobe Reader.

How it works...

We have just converted a file into a PDF. As we embed it, we need to work with some code. We are going to create an activity, in this case create an **Online text** activity, you can choose any other. These are the steps to follow:

1. Click on **Add an activity | Online text** within **Assignments**.

2. Complete the **Assignment name** block.

3. Complete the **Description** block. In this block, highlight some words and click on **Insert /edit link** icon.

4. Click on **Browse** within **Link URL block**.

5. Click on **Upload a file | Browse | Choose the file | Open | Upload this file | Insert**.

6. A link to the PDF file was just created.

7. Click on **HTML** icon. Write the following code:

    ```
    <embed src="FullScreenEmbed.pdf" width="800" height="500">
    ```

8. Change this code with some information. That is to say, add the name of the file just uploaded, instead of `FullScreenEmbed.pdf`, as follows:

    ```
    <embed src="http://localhost/draftfile.php/13/user/
    draft/387786865/Yeti_and_Bigfoot.pdf"width="800" height="500">
    ```

9. Click on **Update**.

10. Click on **Save and display**. It looks as shown in the following screenshot:

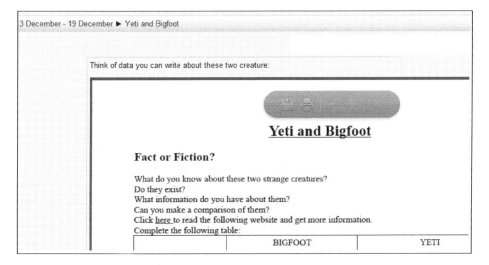

See also

▸ *Reviewing PDF documents*

Reviewing PDF documents

We have worked with PDF documents in the previous recipe. Therefore, use the comments on them. You can review PDF documents in two different ways: add sticky notes or highlight some text. In case you do not want to use Adobe Reader, Open Office and Microsoft Word also provide reviewing facilities, so these are other options to bear in mind.

Getting ready

We need to work with Adobe Reader as well in this recipe. Use the file that has been worked with in the previous two recipes so as to avoid creating a new file. Why should we add some comments? So as to guide students on how to complete a chart and add comments to a piece of writing, among other ideas.

How to do it...

The aim of the recipe is to focus on the way to add comments to the PDF file; therefore, we are not dealing with the document but how to review it. We are covering the two ways to review a file; we can also combine them in order to use both the tools. Enter Adobe Reader and open a file. Follow these steps:

1. Click on **Highlight text** icon, as shown in the following screenshot. Select the text that you want to highlight.

2. Click on **Add sticky note** icon, as shown in the following screenshot:

3. Add a comment to the sticky note.

How it works...

On the right-side of the document, you can see the words that you have highlighted and the sticky notes as well as the comments that were added to the PDF. It is shown in the following screenshot:

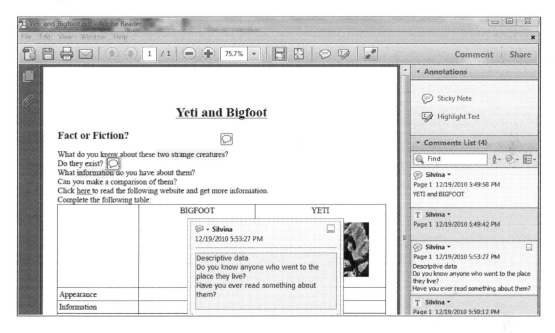

We can add a resource to our Moodle course as done in the previous recipe, therefore, instead of uploading a file from Open Office, upload a `.pdf` file with sticky notes or highlighted comments.

Designing a Wiki

Another interesting and different way of creating collaborative writing is designing a Wiki using the following website: `http://www.wikispaces`. It enhances students' way of learning. Thus, we, as teachers, use several resources in order to avoid routine. Another option is to use Wikis in Moodle 2.0, which are a bit different from the ones belonging to the previous version.

Getting ready

Click on **Create a free classroom wiki** in the aforementioned site, as shown in the following screenshot:

K-12 Classroom Wikis

If your wiki will be used exclusively for **K–12 education**, you probably came here looking for a wiki on our K-12 Plus plan. These wikis are **free** and **ad-free**, and you can make them **private** for extra security for your students. Classroom wikis also come with a User Creator tool that lets you **open student accounts in bulk** — without student email addresses. Create a free classroom wiki.

How to do it...

When we click the previously mentioned link, we come across the following link where some specific information is required; therefore, follow these steps in order to start designing the Wiki:

1. Complete all the blocks fields, as shown in the following screenshot:

2. Another page appears, click on username, in this case **silvinahillar**, in order to start designing the Wiki.

3. Click on **New Page**, on the left margin, as shown circled in the following screenshot:

4. Complete the **Page Name** and **Add Tags** blocks. Then, the **New Page URL** is given underneath these blocks.

5. Click on **Create**.

6. An editor appears in order to create the Wiki. The editor is shown in the following screenshot:

7. The editor is similar to any editor that we have been working with, the only different item to give special attention to is **Widget**. When clicking on the said icon, the following are the widgets that can be added to our Wiki, as shown in the following screenshot:

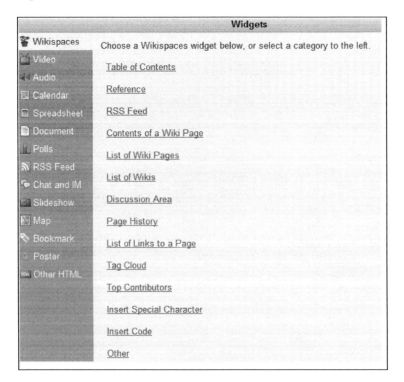

8. We can add any of these previously shown widgets in our Wiki. The instructions are shown when we click on any of these items. Many multimedia assets can easily be uploaded to the wiki.

9. After designing the Wiki, click on **Preview**, in case you want to **edit** something. When ready, click on **Save**.

 There are plenty of features that could take a whole chapter to be explored, though it is not the aim of the book, it is just to let you know how to design a Wiki using a website.

How it works...

We have just designed our Wiki. It is time to embed it in our Moodle course. We can design either an activity or create a resource because the Wiki that we have just created is part of an activity. Students should also write their opinions after discussing with their classmates. Therefore, follow these steps in order to use this Wiki in our virtual classroom:

1. Click on the Wiki that you have just created | **Manage Wiki**.

2. Click on **Badges** within **Tools**.

3. Choose the badge that you want to insert and copy the HTML code.

4. It is time to start our Moodle course. Click on **Add an activity | Offline activity** within **Assignments**.

5. Complete the **Assignment name** and **Description** blocks.

6. Click on the **HTML** icon and paste the code. Therefore, create the activity by pasting the HTML code and inserting the badge.

7. Click on **Save and display**.

8. The activity looks as shown in the following screenshot:

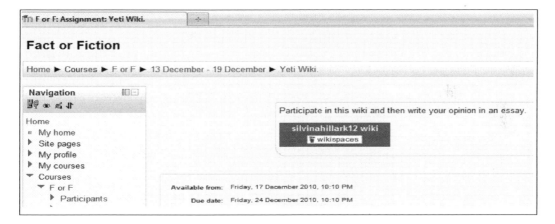

5
Working with Audio, Sound, Music, and Podcasts

In this chapter, we will cover:

- ▶ Recording audio using a microphone
- ▶ Creating and embedding a podcast
- ▶ Creating MP3 files from diverse audio formats
- ▶ Embedding free sound available on the Internet
- ▶ Working with MIDI music
- ▶ Editing MIDI files
- ▶ Embedding playlists in a Moodle activity

Introduction

This chapter explains how to work with different types of audio files to include sounds, music, and podcasts to Moodle courses. These recipes will teach you how to use different tools to record, edit, and convert different audio file formats, covering common scenarios for multimedia Moodle activities.

The sense of hearing plays an important role for effective learning due to the fact that there are plenty of students whose ability to learn depends on their musical intelligence. Besides, inserting this type of ingredient into our activities makes them more interesting to our students.

You can combine several pieces of recording with not only our own voice, but also with somebody else's speaking or sounds, therefore, podcasts won't be dull for students when they have to listen only to the teacher speaking. The mixture of sounds, audio, and music is interesting because students can listen to small pieces of recordings or music as well as ourselves explaining what they are hearing.

Podcasting is an excellent way to share different elements with students. We can combine parts of recordings to provide our students with facilities to listen like a radio show created by their own teacher, depending on how creative you can be. Once you are confident with podcasts, it can be easily enhanced by them.

Students can record their podcasts too. Some of the skills that students develop by creating podcasts include writing scripts and their listening and speaking skills. They learn how to speak better because they have to pay attention to what they listen to. It would be advisable that students listen to our podcasts first and then make their own.

The baseline topic of this chapter is Music and sounds around the world. Therefore, we will design several types of activities in which we need to use this multimedia element in our recipes. We can combine several types of ingredients to make our recipes quite spicy!

Creating podcasts using different resources available on the Web enhances them further. Therefore, we need to know which are the resources that we can bear in mind in order to use them. One of these resources are the free sounds available on the Web. They can be incorporated into Moodle courses or they can be used in order to create a podcast with different sounds. It all depends on what type of activity you want to design.

The software that we use in the first three recipes in this chapter to create a podcast is Audacity. It is free and open source and works with several Operating Systems (OS). It would be advisable to read the recipes in order because they are designed in such a way that they are threaded to one another.

In some of the recipes, we leave aside Audacity, but this does not mean that it cannot be used in order to combine the audio files that we mention. However, it would become a chapter on Audacity if we go on with said software. We can also add sounds available on the Web to the podcasts. We create Audacity software that cannot edit MIDI files, but TuxGuitar can. It is a free and open source software that supports several OS systems and is a great tool for editing MIDI files. Besides, you can create a TuxGuitar Community account and share files with other users. After signing in, you can upload, download, comment, and rate files. You can also ask for help from the music teacher or work with students with said software, especially music lovers.

We will learn how to allow students to record audio after listening to us speaking. It's time for us to listen to them. Create this type of activity in order to make our virtual classroom more vivid. Thus, students practice other skills, as we have stated before, when they have to record themselves.

Recording audio using a microphone

In this recipe, we will learn how to record our voice using a microphone as well as a software. Therefore, using this software we can not only record live audio, but also convert tapes and records into digital recordings among other features for our Moodle courses. Also, be aware of copyright issues of the material that you are using to be recorded.

Getting ready

As we will record audio from a microphone using the Audacity software, download it from the following website: `http://audacity.sourceforge.net/download/`. Bear in mind that this software works with different OS, therefore, click on the OS that is installed in your computer.

How to do it...

After downloading and installing Audacity onto your computer, record the instructions of an activity or record; something that is more interesting to listen to. For example, as the baseline topic of this chapter is **Sounds and music around the world**, focus on different accents of spoken English. Therefore, follow these steps to design the activity:

1. Start Audacity.

2. Click on the **Record** button within the **Audio Control and Editing Toolbars**, as shown in the following screenshot:

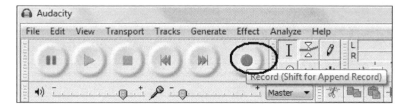

3. When you finish recording, click on the **Stop** button.

4. The digital representation of the voice (wave form) is shown in the audio track portion within the **Project view**, as shown in the following screenshot:

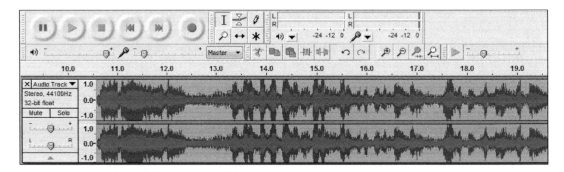

5. Click on **File | Save Project as**, as shown in the following screenshot:

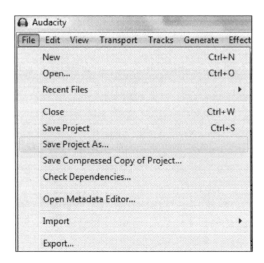

6. Click on **File | Export**, and save the file as **WAV** type. Then, embed the podcast in our Moodle course. It is shown in the following screenshot:

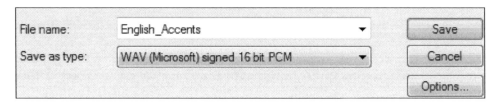

7. Click on **Save | OK**.

How it works...

We need to upload the podcast to our Moodle course. To do this, choose the weekly outline section where you want to insert it and follow these steps:

1. Click on **Add an activity | Online text** within **Assignments**.

2. Complete the **Assignment name** and **Description** blocks.

3. Click on the **Moodle Media** icon | **Find or upload a sound, video or applet... |**
   Upload a file | Browse |. Look for the file that you want to upload and click on it.
   Remember to upload the file with WAV extension; that is to say look for the circled
   icon, as shown in the following screenshot:

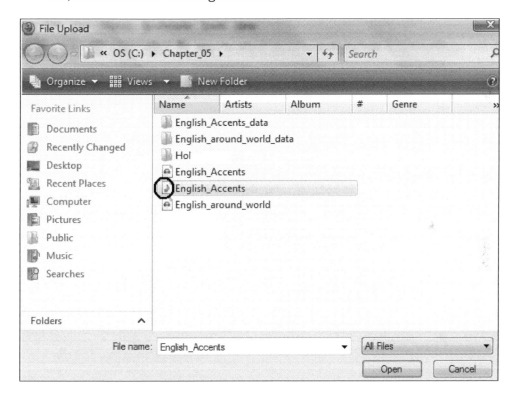

4. Click on **Open | Upload this file | Insert**.

5. Click on **Save and return to course**.

6. Click on the activity. It looks as shown in the following screenshot:

7. When students click on the name of the file, they will see the following media player toolbar, as shown in the following screenshot:

8. When students click on **Play**, they will listen to what we have recorded.

See also

▶ *Creating and embedding a podcast*

Creating and embedding a podcast

In the previous recipe, we learnt how to record ourselves using Audacity (without pausing the recording). If we want to create a podcast for our Moodle course, we can not only record our voice, but also add some music or sound to it in order to enhance it. This is what this task is about.

Getting ready

Combine recordings of people speaking in their native English after describing its characteristics, ask for help from a Linguistic or Phonetics teacher. You can add this element if you happen to have it recorded. You can also add some sounds, for example for the presentation and ending of the podcast as well.

How to do it...

We will work with the Audacity software, which is used in the previous recipe. We can record ourselves as we did before, and convert some parts of tapes, CDs, and MP3 files where we can find the different types of English spoken around the world such as RP English, Creole, Caribbean English, American English among others. Always bear in mind the copyright issues of the material to be recorded. To design the podcast, follow these steps:

1. Start Audacity.
2. Click on the **Record** button within the **Audio Control and Editing Toolbars** in order to record your voice.
3. Click on the **Stop** button before inserting the extra material to enhance the podcast.
4. Click on **File | Import | Audio |** select the file, and click on **Open**.

5. Two waveforms appear in separate audio track portions within the **Project view**. Click on the second waveform and move the **Selection boundary** from the beginning to the end in order to select it, as shown in the following screenshot:

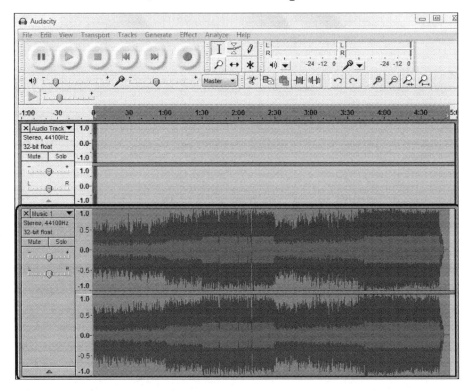

6. Click on **Edit | Cut** (another option is the keys *Ctrl + X*).

7. Place the cursor at the end of the waveform in the first **Project view** and click on **Edit | Paste** (another option is the keys *Ctrl + V*). It looks as shown in the following screenshot:

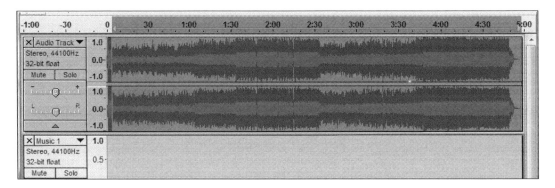

8. Click on **File | Save Project as** and write a name for the project.

9. Click on **File | Export** to save the file as **WAV** type so that you can embed the podcast in the Moodle course.

10. Click on **Save | OK**.

11. You can repeat steps 2 to 7 as many times as you want if you want to go on recording your voice or add extra audio files.

How it works...

When we upload this podcast to our Moodle course, we can listen to it without pauses because we have just created a podcast that was combined with another source of audio, sound, or music. That is to say that we have learnt how to cope with different sounds in order to design one recording. Those parts of the songs, sounds, or just phrases that we want our students to listen to can be shared when designing a podcast for any activity.

This is a great tool suitable for any subject. Thus, the combination of sounds, music, and audio make our podcast less dull and more appealing through the variety of content. It can sometimes be boring to listen to the same person speaking all the time.

See also

▶ *Recording audio using a microphone*

Creating MP3 files from diverse audio formats

It is because of the MP3 that it is one of the most amazing phenomena that enables us to create files smaller in size without putting aside sound quality of different audio sources. So, we focus on creating this type of file in this chapter. The MP3 format for digital audio has an enormous impact on people collecting, listening, and distributing different sources of audio recordings.

Getting ready

The MP3 format is a compression system for music. Thus, the aim of the recipe is to create this type of file in order to make it possible to store several audio sources in different recordings that we want to upload to our Moodle courses.

The MP3 format is a lossy compression system, that is to say that there are certain sounds that we cannot hear, or we hear certain sounds better than others; especially when two sounds are playing simultaneously, we can hear the louder one. Thus, this type of compression eliminates what we cannot hear properly. In order to create this type of file, use Audacity.

How to do it...

We have already used Audacity in the previous recipes. Therefore, we are getting familiar with the said software. In this recipe, we will create MP3 files from diverse audio formats. Create an activity in which students can listen to Caribbean English. These are the steps to follow:

1. Start Audacity.

2. Click on **File | Import | Audio |**, browse for the file that you want to open, and click on it | **Open**.

3. Click on **File | Export**. A pop-up window appears. Choose MP3 Files, as shown in the following screenshot:

4. Click on **Save**.

5. There appears a pop-up window in which you can complete the following information about the recording, as shown in the following screenshot:

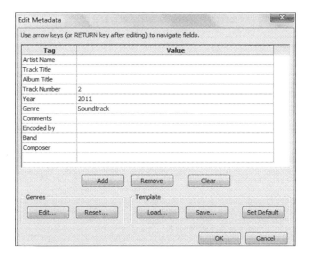

6. Click **OK**.

How it works...

We have just converted an audio file to MP3. Combine different audio sources and create one podcast. The recipes in this chapter are designed in such a way that they are linked to one another, therefore, follow these three recipes and create a wonderful podcast in an MP3 format because it is smaller in size. In the following screenshot, compare the same file saved in different formats, and pay attention to the size in both cases. The screenshot on the left is a .WAV and the one on the right is an MP3 file:

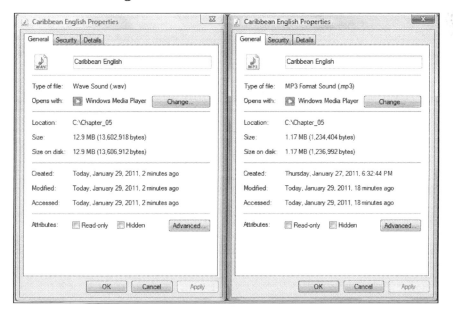

Upload it to our Moodle course as we have already done so before. Just click on the **Moodle Media** icon and upload the file as we did in the first recipe.

See also

▶ *Recording audio from a microphone*

▶ *Creating and embedding a podcast*

Embedding free sound available on the Web

It is time we paid attention to the free sound available on the Web that can be useful to enhance our podcasts. A useful website where you can find a wide variety of sound is `http://www.freesound.org/`. **The Freesound Project** website offers sound with a Creative Commons License. It only contains sound; you won't find any songs because most of them are protected by copyright.

Getting ready

Visit the aforementioned website and click on **Join** because it is necessary to register in order to download its files. Both the registration and access to its content are free of cost. Therefore, on the left-hand margin, click on **Join / Register** and complete the necessary information. Bear in mind that this website does not work with Hotmail accounts because of problems with the said service. Therefore, log in with another e-mail provider, for example Gmail or Yahoo!. This information is shown in the following screenshot:

How to do it...

Search for files to work with, find some sounds related to some countries or sounds of the nature and mention where we can find them. We can accept a great variety of answers, or just design a guessing activity with sound clues. Thus, focus on one country and add as many sounds as possible for students to guess which country we are describing through the sound. Follow these steps to find some sound files:

1. Click on **Search** under **Search / Browse** on the left-hand margin.

2. Activate the **Filenames** checkbox so that the website searches for the filenames of its sound files database.

3. Enter the sound that you want to look for and click on **Submit**.

4. Click the **Play** button and listen to the recorded sound, as shown in the following screenshot:

5. After listening to the results, click on the file that suits you. A new page with more detailed information appears, as shown in the following screenshot:

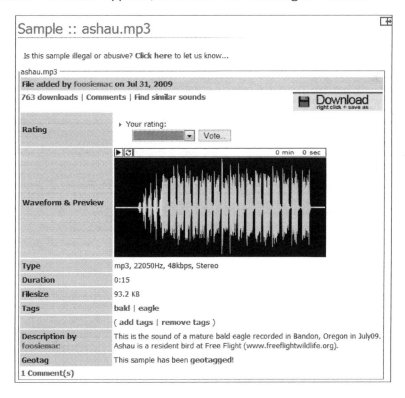

6. After checking the license information of the chosen file, right-click on the **Download** icon. The context menu appears; click on **Save Target As**, as shown in the following screenshot:

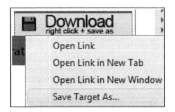

7. Name and save the file.

8. If you want to download other sounds, repeat steps 1-7.

How it works...

We can enhance any type of activity using sound. In this case, add a **Chat** to our course in which students are to discuss which country we are describing through the sounds. Upload it to our Moodle course, as we have already done so before. Just click on the **Moodle Media** icon and upload the file as we did in the first recipe.

If we want to create a podcast in which we combine the sounds that we have downloaded with our voice, we can do it using Audacity software, as we did in the previous recipes. In the case that the file that we have chosen in the previous website is not an .mp3, we can convert it as we did in the previous recipe using Audacity as well.

See also

▶ *Recording audio using a microphone*

▶ *Creating and embedding a podcast*

▶ *Creating MP3 files from diverse audio formats*

Working with MIDI music

The digitalization of the sound is not the only function of a sound card; it also has the ability to produce sounds electronically through a synthesizer incorporated in the card compatible with **MIDI (Musical Instruments Digital Interface)** files. MIDI files have instructions that indicate to the sound card synthesizer the musical note, intervals, the musical instrument among other features that it will use so that the synthesizer generates the corresponding sound.

In this way, the size of a file that has a complete note reading as MIDI files is a thousand times smaller than a file that contains the digitalized note reading. Furthermore, its modifications are easier in MIDI files. Games among other multimedia applications use MIDI in order to reproduce their melodies.

We can connect a piano keyboard if the sound card supports MIDI to transmit commands to the MIDI port (the same used for the old-fashioned joystick). We have to bear in mind that we can connect some keyboards to a USB port, instead of using the MIDI port.

Getting ready

We can find MIDI files at the following website: `http://mididb.com/`. You can search for the music that you need to design your activity.

How to do it...

You can find several MIDI files in this website by clicking on the upper ribbon. Therefore, we will search for National Anthems of English-speaking countries around the world in order to use these files to create the activity in our Moodle course:

1. Visit the `http://mididb.com/` website.

2. Click on **Themes | National Anthems** on the upper ribbon.

3. Choose the Anthem that you want to upload. Right-click on it and choose **Save Link As...**, as shown in the following screenshot:

4. Click on **Save**. You can save other MIDI files following steps 2-4.

How it works...

Create an activity in which students listen to different Anthems of different English-speaking countries. Afterwards, they have to complete a chart adding more information about each of those countries. Therefore, to add this activity, follow these steps:

1. Click on **Add an activity | Upload a single file** within **Assignments**.

2. Complete the **Assignment Name** and **Description** blocks.

3. Click on the **Moodle Media** icon | **Find or upload a sound, video or applet...** | **Upload a file** | **Browse** |. Look for the MIDI file that you want to upload and click on it.

4. Click on **Open** | **Upload this file** | **Insert**.

5. Click on **Save and return to course**. Click on the activity. It looks as shown in the following screenshot:

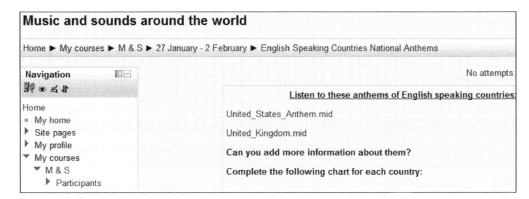

See also

▶ *Editing MIDI files*

Editing MIDI files

In the previous recipe, we found MIDI files available on the Web. Therefore, it is time to edit them. So, search in the previous website for files to edit or we can find them in TuxGuitar (http://tuxguitar.com.ar/) with which we will work. Choose to edit any song, but bear in mind the copyright issues.

Getting ready

We will edit MIDI files using the software that we have mentioned before. Therefore, download the software at http://tuxguitar.com.ar/download.html. This software supports several OS, so choose yours accordingly. TuxGuitar is a multitrack tablature editor and player; using it, we can compose music. Some of its features are tablature editor, score viewer, multitrack display, among others.

How to do it...

Run the said software. A pop-up window appears where you can click in order to join the TuxGuitar community, as shown in the following screenshot:

Go back to the said software and follow these steps in order to edit MIDI files:

1. Click on **File | Import | Import MiDi**, as shown in the following screenshot:

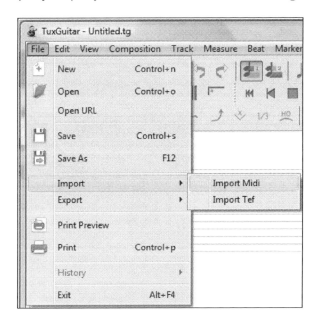

2. Search for the MIDI file that you want to edit. Click on the file | **Open** | **OK**.

3.   When you open the file, it looks as shown in the following screenshot:

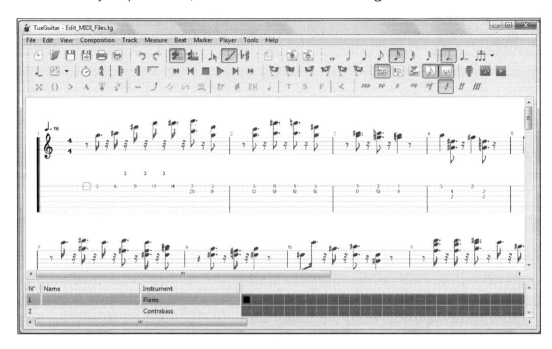

4.   The reading notes appear, and when you click on the instrument you can see it in the underneath part.

5.   You can edit the MIDI file, clicking on the notes that appear on the upper ribbon and add them to the existing one, as shown in the following screenshot:

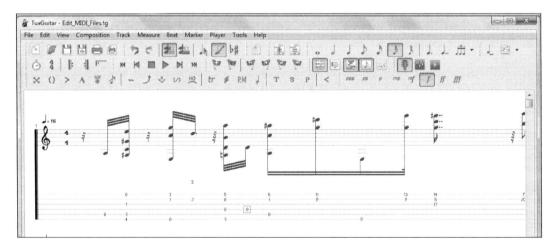

6. Click on **View**, and within that option you can choose from a range of options to show different tools. To show / display tools (in pop-up windows), tick any/all of the following: **Show Mixer, Show Player, Show Fretboard, Show Piano, Show Matrix**. All are shown in the following screenshot:

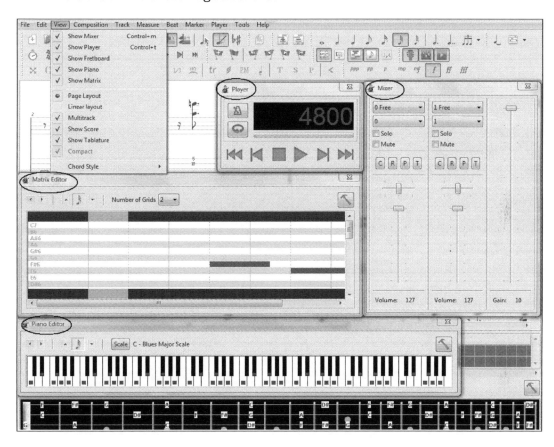

7. When you are done, save the file. Click on **File | Save as** and write a name for the edited MIDI.

How it works...

Before uploading it to Moodle, listen to it in order to check what we have just done! Afterwards, choose the weekly outline section where you want to add the activity or the resource, and upload the file, as done in the previous recipes.

It would be advisable that students install TuxGuitar because when we save the changes to the MIDI files, they appear with the extension of the said software otherwise, they will not be able to open the file.

Allowing students to record audio

This is a very simple recipe that can be carried out using Moodle assignments; that is to say through uploading files. It means that students are going to record themselves and we can listen to them through the file that they upload. We can set guidelines as we do when writing, with respect to their speaking.

Getting ready

It is time for our students to take a deep breath and talk. Therefore, clearly mention what we want to hear from them. Ask students to talk about the type of English they speak according to what they have heard before in the podcasts that we have created.

How to do it...

Students can record themselves using either devices such as their mobile phones or the Audacity software for creating podcasts. We should ask them to upload .mp3 files, as well as other important guidelines such as time and information. Follow these steps to design the activity:

1. Click on **Add an activity | Upload a single file** within **Assignments**.
2. Complete the **Assignment name** and **Description** blocks. Set the guidelines clearly so that students know what they have to record.

3. In the **Maximum size** within the **Upload a single file** block, choose **16MB**, as shown in the following screenshot:

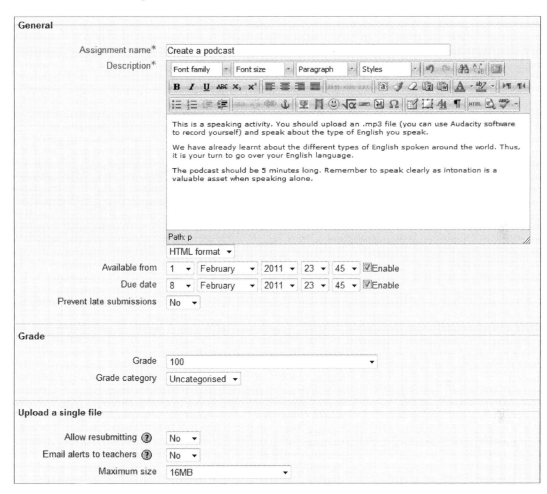

4. Click on **Save and return to course**.

How it works...

When students submit their answers and we click on the file that they have uploaded in order to grade them, just click on it and listen. The file created by the students appears as shown in the following screenshot:

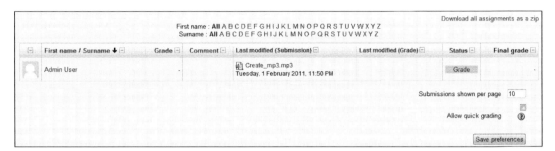

6

Creating and Integrating Screencasts and Videos

In this chapter, we will cover:

- ► Creating a screencast
- ► Enhancing a screencast with annotations
- ► Embedding a YouTube video
- ► Embedding a Dailymotion video
- ► Recording a video
- ► Editing a video
- ► Creating a playlist
- ► Enhancing a video with comments

Introduction

This chapter explains how to create screencasts and edit them, as well as link and embed videos for our Moodle courses. The recipes use diverse free and open source multi-platform tools to record, edit, and convert the different video files, covering the most common scenarios for multimedia Moodle activities.

Besides, Moodle 2.0 offers new features, which make it easier to insert videos, especially from the http://www.youtube.com website. You can find them easily from the file picker, provided you have administrative access to the course. You have to bear in mind that you need to be an administrator in order to enable this option.

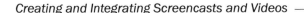

It covers different ways to create and interact using either screencasts or videos. We will work with several multimedia assets, which will concern the baseline topic of Wildlife. This topic has many resources, which can be integrated with screencasts and videos available on the Web.

Creating screencasts using several free and open source software available on the Web is one of the main goals of this chapter. There is plenty of commercial software, which can be used to create screencasts. We will not focus on them though. We add some special features to the screencasts in order to enhance them.

Videos can be recorded in several ways. You may use your cell phone, camera, or the webcam of your computer. We are to focus on the way of creating them and uploading into our Moodle course. We can also use a recorded video from YouTube and upload it directly from the file picker in Moodle 2.0.

You can also design a playlist in order to combine several videos and let your students watch them in a row. We do it by creating an account in YouTube. The channel in YouTube can be either public or private; it depends on how we want to carry it out.

You can create some screencasts in order to present information to your students instead of showing presentations made using Open Office, PowerPoint, or Microsoft Word. Changing any of these into a screencast is more appealing to the students and not such a difficult task to carry out either.

We can create an explanation by recording our voice, for which we will create a virtual board that we can choose to be visible to the audience; in the second case, our explanations can only be heard with no visualization. This is quite an important aspect to be taken into account, especially in teaching because students need a dynamic explanation by their teacher.

There are several software available that can be used to create screencasts. One of them is **Cam Studio**. This software captures AVI files and it is open source. It captures onscreen video and audio. Its disadvantage is that only Windows users can use it. You can download it from `http://camstudio.com/`.

It is time for Mac users. There is also a free program for Mac users that focuses on making quick films by saving the recorded video to get a quick access. It does not record audio. This is Copernicus and you can download it from `http://danicsoft.com/software/copernicus/`.

We need a tool for both Mac and Windows, which is free and open source as well. So, JingProject.com is the software. It does not only record video, but also allows you to take a picture, draw, or add a message on it, and upload the media to a free hosting account. A URL is provided in order to watch the video or the image. You can download it from the following website: `http://www.techsmith.com/download/jing/`.

Screencast-o-matic is another tool that is based on Java that does not need to be downloaded at all. It allows you to upload in an automatic way. It works well with both Mac and Windows machines. You can use this at `http://www.screencast-o-matic.com/`. This is the tool that we are to work with in the creation of a screencast.

We may also modify the videos to make them suitable for learning. We can add annotations in different ways so as to interact through the video with our students. That is to say, we add our comments instead of adding our voice so that students read what we need to tell them.

Creating a screencast

In this recipe, we create a screencast and upload it to our Moodle course. The baseline topic is Wildlife. Therefore, in this recipe, we will explain to our students where wild animals are located. We can paste in a world map of the different animals, while we add extra data through the audio files. Thus, we can also add more information using different types of images that are inserted in the map.

Getting ready

Before creating the screencast, plan the whole sequence of the explanation that we want to show to our students, therefore, we will use a very useful Java applet available at `http://www.screencast-o-matic.com/`.

Screencast-o-matic requires the free Java Run-time Environment (also known as JRE) for both the teacher and the students' computers. You can download and install its latest version from `http://java.sun.com`.

How to do it...

First of all, design the background scene of the screencast to work with. Afterwards, enter the website `http://www.screencast-o-matic.com/`. Follow these to create the screencast:

1. Click on **Start recording**.

2. Another pop-up window appears that looks as shown in the following screenshot:

3. Resize the frame to surround the recording area that you want to record.

4. Click on the recording button (red button).

5. If you want to make a pause, click on the pause button or *Alt + P*, as shown in the following screenshot:

6. If you want to integrate the webcam or a bluetooth video, click on the upwards arrow in this icon, as shown in the following screenshot:

7. When the screencast is finished, click on **Done**.

8. You can preview the screencast after you finish designing it. If you need to edit it, click on **Go back to add more**. If you are satisfied with the preview, click on **Done with this screencast**, as shown in the following screenshot:

9. When the screencast is finished, our next task is to export it because we need to upload it to our Moodle course. Click on **Export Movie**.

10. Click on the downwards arrow in **Type** and choose **Flash (FLV)**, as shown in the following screenshot:

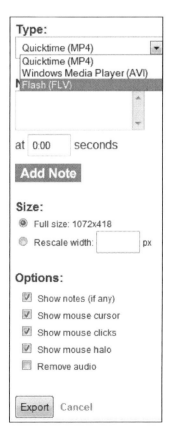

11. Customize the **Size** and **Options** blocks, as shown in the previous screenshot or as you wish. When you finish, click on **Export**, as shown in the previous screenshot.

12. Write a name for this file and click on **Save**.

13. When the file is exported, click on **Go back and do more with this screencast** if you want to edit it.

14. Click on **Done with this screencast** if you are satisfied with the result. A pop-up window appears, click on **OK**.

How it works...

We have just created the screencast teaching about wild animals, which students have to watch to learn about the places where wild animals live around the world. We need to upload it to our Moodle course. It is a passive resource; therefore, we can add a resource or design an activity out of it. In this case, we design an activity. Choose the weekly outline section where you want to insert it, and follow these steps:

1. Click on **Add an activity | Online text** within **Assignments**.

2. Complete the **Assignment name** and **Description** blocks.

3. Click on the **Moodle Media** icon | **Find or upload a sound, video or applet ...** | **Upload a file** | **Browse** | look for the file that you want to upload and click on it.

4. Click on **Open | Upload this file | Insert**.

5. Click on **Save and return to course**.

6. Click on the activity. It looks as shown in the following screenshot:

There's more...

In the case that we create a screencast, which lasts for around 30 minutes or longer, it will take a long time to upload it to our Moodle course. Therefore, it will be advisable to watch the screencast using a free and open source media player, that is to say VLC Media Player.

VLC Media Player

You can download the VLC Media Player from the following website: `http://www.videolan.org/vlc/`. It works with most popular video files formats such as AVI, MP4, and Flash, among others. Follow these steps in order to watch the screencast:

1. Click on **Media** | **Open File** | browse for the file that you want to open and click on it.

2. Click on **Open**. The screencast is displayed, as shown in the following screenshot:

See also

▶ *Enhancing a screencast with annotations*

Enhancing a screencast with annotations

We have already created a screencast in the previous recipe. Therefore, we can design another one about a specific wild animal and write some text at the specified seconds. Those texts are to be the annotations that we can add to our screencast.

Getting ready

In the previous task, we have already used `http://www.screencast-o-matic.com/`, and we will use this software in order to add the annotations to the new screencast that we will create in this recipe.

How to do it...

Enter the previously-mentioned website and follow these steps in order to create a screencast enhanced with annotations:

1. Click on **Start recording** and resize the frame to surround the recording area that you want to record.

2. Click on the recording button to record the screencast.

3. When the screencast is finished, click on **Done | Done with this screencast | Export Movie**.

4. Click on the downwards arrow in **Type** and choose **Flash (FLV)**.

5. Play the screencast. Write the annotations that you want to add within the **Note** block. Click on **Add Note** when the screencast is being played at the second that you wish to add the annotations, as shown in the following screenshot:

6. Customize the **Size** and **Options** blocks. When you finish, click on **Export**.

7. Write a name for this file and click on **Save**.

8. Click on **Done with this screencast** if you are satisfied with the result. A pop-up window appears, click **OK**.

How it works...

We have already designed the screencast that students have to watch to learn one of the reasons why the panda bear is endangered. Upload it to our Moodle course. Choose the weekly outline section where you want to insert it and follow these steps:

1. Click on **Add an activity | Upload a single file** within **Assignments**.

2. Complete the **Assignment name** and **Description** blocks.

3. Click on the **Moodle Media** icon | **Find or upload a sound, video or applet ...** | **Upload a file** | **Browse** | Look for the file that you want to upload and click on it.

4. Click on **Open** | **Upload this file** | **Insert**.

5. Click on **Save and return to course**. Click on the activity. It looks as shown in the following screenshot:

See also

▶ *Creating a screencast*

Embedding a YouTube video

Moodle 2.0 offers the possibility to add YouTube within the file picker when we want to upload some media files to enhance our Moodle courses. Therefore, in this recipe we will consider the fact to make this visible in the file picker.

Getting ready

There are some steps that you need to take into account in order to enable the YouTube options in the file picker.

How to do it...

Let's switch our role in order to enable YouTube videos, available from the file picker. Therefore, click on **Switch role to** and select **Manager**. After switching your role, these are the steps to follow:

1. Click on **Site administration | Plugins | Repositories | Manage repositories**.

2. Click on next to **YouTube videos Enabled and visible**, as shown in the following screenshot:

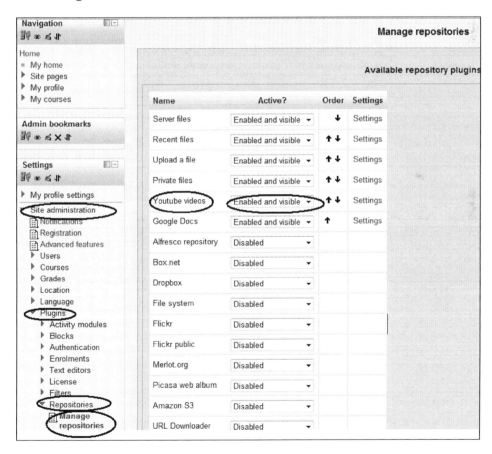

3. Click on **Save | Save changes**.

How it works...

We have just enabled YouTube videos to be shown in the file picker whenever we want to upload a video from the said website in our Moodle course. So, these are the steps to follow:

1. Click on **Add an activity | Upload a single file** within **Assignments**.
2. Complete the **Assignment name** and **Description** blocks.
3. Click on the **Moodle Media** icon | **Find or upload a sound, video or applet ... |** **Youtube videos**.
4. Complete the **Search videos** block with the video that you want to look for, as shown in the following screenshot:

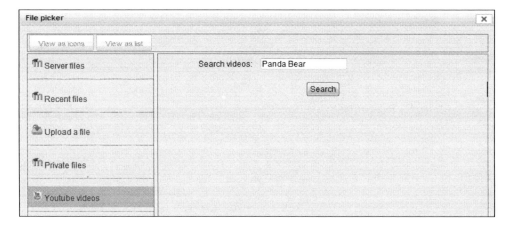

5. Click on **Search**.
6. Many videos appear containing the said word. You click on the one that you want to embed, as shown in the following screenshot:

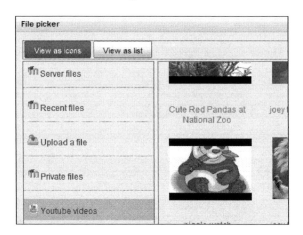

7. You can choose between **View as icons** or **View as list**. The **View as icons** is shown in the previous screenshot.

8. Click on **Select this file**.

9. It is advisable to play the video before embedding it in the Moodle course. So, click on play and watch the video, as shown in the following screenshot:

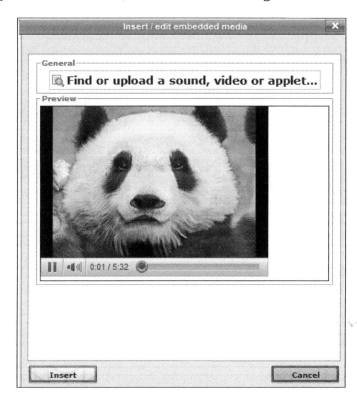

10. Click on **Insert** if you are happy with the video.

11. Click on **Save and return to course**. The video is embedded in our Moodle course.

Embedding a Dailymotion video

This recipe is very simple. You can also find interesting videos at the following website: `http://www.dailymotion.com/us`. It is an alternative to YouTube if you want to find some more videos about a certain topic.

Getting ready

Enter the previously-mentioned website. In the **Search** block, write the words related to the video that you want to look for. In this case, leave the panda aside and look for a video of the bald eagle, as shown in the following screenshot:

How to do it...

After searching for the videos, select the one that we want to embed in our Moodle course. So, follow these steps to find the embedding code:

1. Click on the video that you want to embed.

2. Click on **Embed** and copy the embed code within the **Copy Embed Code** block, as shown in the following screenshot:

3. You can also adjust the **Settings** as you wish, as shown in the previous screenshot on the right-hand side.

How it works...

Embed this video either as a resource or as a warm up in an activity. Therefore, enter the weekly outline section where you want to add this resource. These are the steps to follow:

1. Click on **Add a resource | Page**.
2. Complete the **Name** and **Description** blocks.
3. Complete the **Page Content** block.
4. Click on the **Edit HTML Source** icon. Paste the HTML code that you had copied from the Dailymotion video website. Click on **Update**.
5. Click on **Save and return to course**. Click on the activity; it looks as shown in the following screenshot:

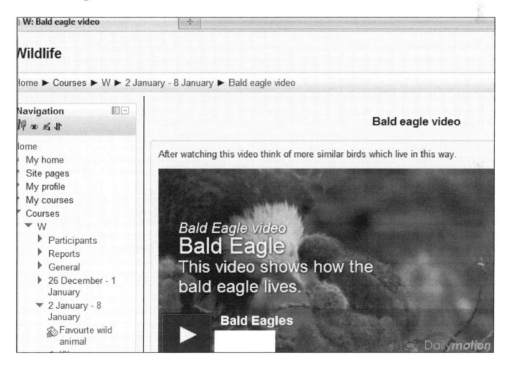

Recording a video

In this recipe, we will record a video. In this case, we record a visit to the zoo because, in this chapter, we deal with wildlife. Therefore, we may have a video from a visit to the zoo, or any park that we might have once visited. Thus, in this case, a mobile camera will be the most suitable.

How to do it...

Use a 720p HD video. It is a video from a visit to a national park in which we can find several wild animals. In order to watch the video on our computer, we need to have installed VLC Media Player. We have already used it in the previous recipe. This software will allow us to watch the video that we have just recorded and its properties. Follow these steps to record a video and save it in your computer:

1. Record the video.

2. Connect the video recorder to the computer. Click on **Open the folder to view files**.

3. Select the video that you want to watch. Right-click on the video. Click on **Copy**.

4. Create a folder on your default web browser and paste the video on the said folder.

5. Save the video that you want to work with.

6. Using VLC Media Player, open the files that you have just saved. Click on **Media | Open File |** choose the file that you need to open, as shown in the following screenshot:

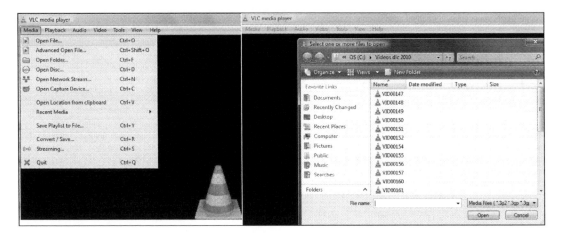

7. Click on the file | **Open**.

8. The video that you chose will be played.

How it works...

Upload the video that we have just recorded to our Moodle course. We can create a chat room in our Moodle course to add some social interaction and let our students discuss the video among themselves. Choose the weekly outline section where we want to add this activity and follow these steps:

1. Click on **Add an activity | Chat**.

2. Complete the **Name of this chat room** and **Introduction text** blocks.

3. Click on the **Moodle Media** icon | **Find or upload a sound, video or applet ...** | **Upload a file** | **Browse** | look for the file that you want to upload and click on it.

4. Click on **Open | Upload this file | Insert**.

5. Click on **Save and return to course**. Click on the activity. It looks as shown in the following screenshot:

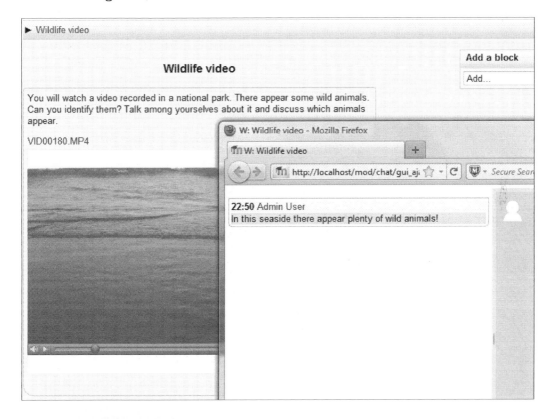

See also

▶   *Creating a screencast*

Editing a video

In order to edit a video, we will use VLMC. We can either cut the video or enlarge it using another one. Therefore, in this recipe we work on both of these items. We will remove a part of the video that we recorded and we enlarge it using another video. That is to say, we can combine two or more videos for our students; we can use a video from the Web and combine it with another of our creation.

Getting ready

In this recipe, we will edit a video using VLMC. We can edit the video that we have just recorded or choose any other video. Therefore, we need to download the software at `http://trac.videolan.org/vlmc`. This software runs with Windows, Linux, and Mac OS.

How to do it...

Click on the VLMC icon and run it. Follow these steps to edit this video:

1. Click on **File | Import |** and browse for the video to edit.
2. Click on the video | click on the arrow (that is circled), and the file appears in the **Media list** block, as shown in the following screenshot:

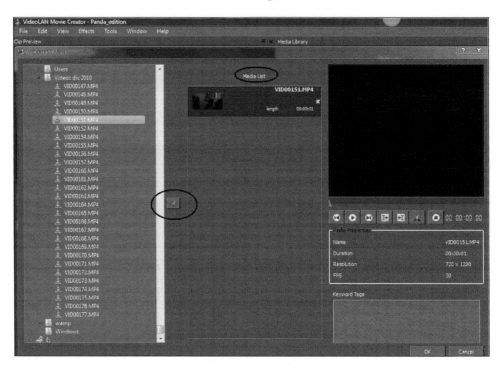

3. Click on **OK**.

4. Click on **Play** within the **Clip Preview** block. The video will be played.

5. When you watch the part that you need, click on the left square bracket, and when that part finishes, click on the right square bracket within the **Clip Preview**, as shown in the following screenshot:

6. Click on the arrow that appears next to the file within the **Media List** block, as shown in the following screenshot:

7.   Drag-and-drop the video to the section shown in the following screenshot:

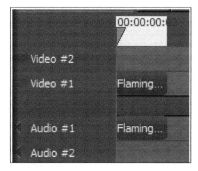

8.   Click on **File** | **Render** | **OK**.

9.   Repeat the same process as many times as you want. You can either use the parts of the same video or you can import another one.

10. When you finish the editing, save the file.

How it works...

After we have edited our video, we can upload it to our Moodle course. Before uploading it to Moodle, we can watch it using VLC Media Player. Afterwards, choose the weekly outline section where you want to add the activity or the resource, and we can upload the video to our Moodle course, as we have already done in the previous recipes.

Creating a playlist

We can create a playlist so that instead of showing one video to our students, we can show them several videos. It is not very difficult to do, but in order to create a playlist, we do need to take a previous step: create an account on YouTube.

Getting ready

Enter YouTube. Click on the **Create Account** icon and complete the necessary information, as shown in the following screenshot:

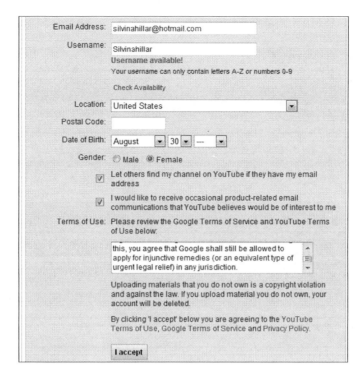

How to do it...

After filling all the information in the last screenshot, and reading all the terms and conditions, click on the **I accept** icon and then follow these steps:

1. Write a password in order to sign in to your account. Then, click on **Sign in**, as shown in the following screenshot:

2. When you are signed in, click on **Browse** | complete the **Search** block with the items that you need to look for, for instance National Geographic Channel wild animals.

3. You can choose a video to upload in our channel. Click on the downwards arrow in your user's name and choose **My Videos**.

4. On the left-hand margin, there appears **Playlist + New**. Click on **+ New**, and complete the pop-up window that appears, as shown in the following screenshot:

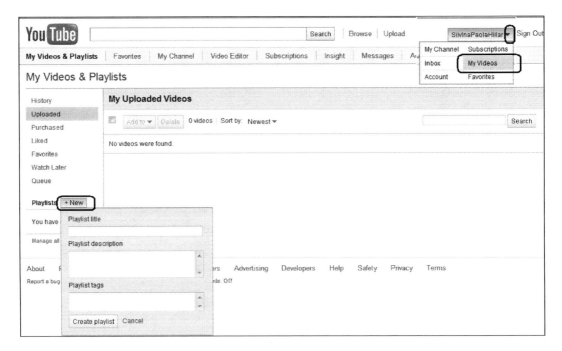

5. Click on the downwards arrow in the **Add videos to playlist** block. There will appear the history of videos that you have watched, therefore, if you want to add them to our playlist, click on **Add**, as shown in the following screenshot:

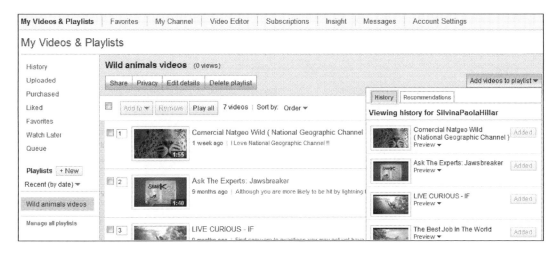

6. The videos added are shown on the left.

How it works...

We have already created a playlist. When we want to watch the playlist of videos, they are displayed one after the other. Thus, enter your channel and click on the name of the playlist that we have just created. Click on **Play all**, and all the videos will be played. The videos belonging to the playlist are displayed underneath the video being broadcast in the playlist bar. The playlist bar allows the viewer to browse through videos without leaving the watch page, as shown in the following screenshot:

If you want to **Turn autoplay off** or **Shuffle videos**, click on the following icons in the playlist bar:

There's more

Embed the playlist in our Moodle course. We would like our students to watch the videos in a row. In order to design this type of resource, we have to copy the embedding code of the playlist.

Uploading a playlist in Moodle

In order to get the embedding code of the playlist, click on the name of the playlist that we have created and follow these steps:

1. Click on **Play all**.

2. Click on **Options | More information about this playlist**, as shown in the following screenshot:

3. Click on **Embed** to get the embedding code for this playlist, as shown in the following screenshot:

4. Copy the code and embed it into our Moodle course either as a resource or an activity. When embedded in the Moodle course (clicking on the **HTML** icon), there appear two arrows next to videos. Thus, the playlist looks as shown in the following screenshot:

Enhancing a video with comments

We can also enhance videos that we want our students to watch with comments. For that reason, we need to again use the channel that we have created on YouTube. We upload the video that we have edited to our account and we enhance it with comments in our account.

Getting ready

First of all, we need to choose the video to which we will add comments, and we have to think about the information that we want to add to it. Therefore, as previously mentioned, we can add comments to the video that we had edited before.

How to do it...

Follow these steps to upload a video:

1. Click on **Upload** (on the top margin) | **Upload a video** (on the left-hand margin).
2. Browse for the video that you want to upload and click on **Open**.
3. You can publish the video as either Public or Private. Therefore, click on the ring button that you desire. Click on **Save changes**.
4. Click on the downwards arrow within your user's name block and choose **My Videos**.
5. All the videos that have been uploaded in the account will appear. Next to the video to which comments are to be added, click on the downwards arrow in the **Insight** block, as shown in the following screenshot:

6. Click on **Annotations**, as shown in the previous screenshot.
7. Within **Annotations**, you can choose to add them among these options: **Speech bubble**, **Note**, **Title**, **Spotlight**, or **Pause**, as shown in the following screenshot:

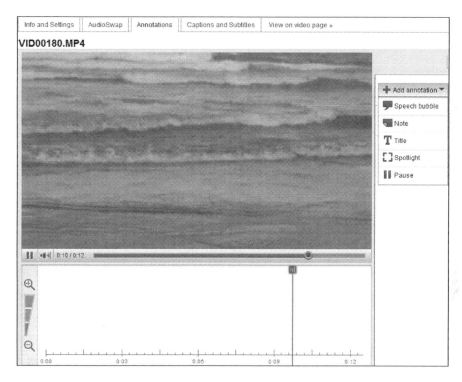

9. You can choose when to add the annotations and the type. After inserting the annotations, click on **Save** | **Publish**, as shown in the following screenshot:

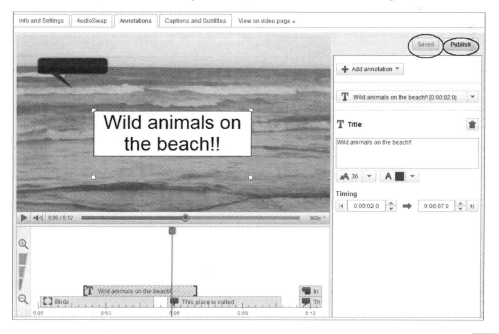

10. You can choose the font color, font size, or background color among other options.

11. You can also change the time period in which the annotation appears, as well as including videos, playlists, and channels among other options.

How it works...

When playing the video, we can read the annotations written in the video. They will be displayed as we have designed them. We can upload the said video to our Moodle course copying the embedding code, as shown in the following screenshot:

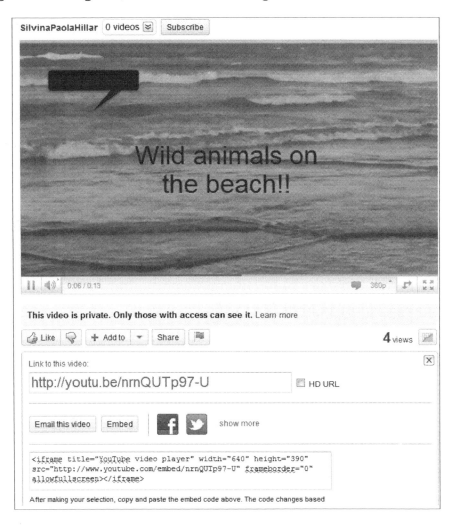

There are also other options available to share this video, such as e-mailing, copying the link, or even using social networks, as shown in the previous screenshot.

7
Working with
Bitmap Images and
Photographs

In this chapter, we will cover:

- ► Selecting between lossy and lossless compression schemes
- ► Creating animated graphics
- ► Resizing photos to their appropriate size
- ► Adding hotspots to photos
- ► Editing color curves
- ► Adding effects and applying filters
- ► Uploading image filters to Moodle
- ► Linking external image files

Introduction

This chapter explains how to work with different types of bitmap image file formats that use lossless and lossy compression schemes. The recipes use diverse tools to edit, enhance, and convert the different image files, covering most scenarios for multimedia Moodle activities that deal with Arts and Photography as a base topic.

Animated graphics are a very important asset to take into account if we want to enhance the look of our Moodle course. We will learn how to create and insert them in Moodle. Activities are much more appealing and engaging with these types of graphics. Thus, we work with a website where we can design them.

Adding elements to the graphics is also an interesting point to take into account when designing an interesting course. We learn how to add hotspots and effects to photos, and apply filters.

After reading this chapter, we will learn how to link, edit, and embed bitmap images and photographs. We will also be able to resize and convert them to the most appropriate formats for Moodle courses. The recipes are designed in such a way that they are all combined.

When thinking of art or photography, we may have the idea of a painter or a photographer in mind, though people who work for these fields may have related jobs such as designing logos for companies or taking pictures for magazines.

Students could upload their images of drawings or design logos for a drawing competition. For instance, some schools happen to be divided into houses that run inter-house competitions. We could design activities in which students vote for the logo of their house or the diagram of the flag.

These were some possibilities for creating social interaction among students using bitmap images and photographs. We are going to learn the best way to upload them to our Moodle course according to what we want to design. Moreover, you can design activities in which you use famous works of art from well-known artists from different times in order to broaden the culture of your students. Additionally, you could interact with a History or Art teacher and develop the understanding of a painting or picture taken at a certain time and explore the history of that period.

Selecting between lossy and lossless compression schemes

When we save a bitmap image, we can choose between lossy and lossless compression schemes to reduce the file size that stores the color information for each pixel that is composed in the bitmap image.

Lossless compression schemes retain all the original color information; and therefore, they keep the original quality, but they produce a large file size. On the other hand, lossy compression schemes replace some color information with approximated values to produce a smaller file size. Thus, lossy compression schemes don't keep the original quality.

In this recipe, we will learn how to choose between one scheme over the other. However, a smaller size is not the only thing that matters!

Getting ready

Capture an image of the map of the Louvre Museum in France in order to use it in our Moodle course. In this case, we contrast both lossy and lossless compression with this map. Save them as .PNG, not as .JPG, because the resolution of a .JPG image is low and is not convenient to work with.

How to do it...

Enter `http://maps.google.com/` and capture the image of the location of the Louvre Museum in France. We have already covered maps in _Chapter 2, Working with 2D and 3D Maps_. We are going to use GIMP. If you do not have it yet, download and install GIMP 2.6.8 (`http://www.gimp.org/downloads/`). Therefore, these are the steps to follow:

1. Enter `http://maps.google.com/` and look for the location of the Louvre Museum in France. You may look for another museum or art gallery if you wish.

2. Press the _Print Screen_ key when you find the location of the museum.

3. Paste the image in GIMP. Click on **Rectangle Select Tool: Select a rectangular region R** and choose the part of the map where the museum is located (you do not need the whole map, as shown in a later screenshot):

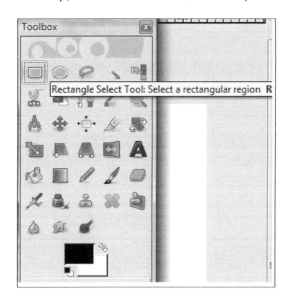

4. Click on **Edit | Cut** and paste the new image in a new document. In fact, you are going to work with two documents. Save the same image with two different extensions.

How it works...

We are going to compare the two files. The image is the same: the part of the map that shows the location of the Louvre Museum in France. What we change is the extension, the type of the image file. We compare the two pictures and they will show that lossless compression is used when it is important that the original and the decompressed bitmap image or photograph be identical. PNG only uses lossless compression.

Remember that we are still working with GIMP. Follow these steps in order to compare both images:

1. Click on **File | Save as ...**.

2. Complete the **Name** field. Type "Louvre_Lossy".

3. Click on the downwards arrow in **All images** at the bottom of the pop-up window and choose **JPEG image**. The image is blurry and pixilated. If you happen to see them in color, they tend to fade away. The more you enlarge the .JPG image, the blurrier it gets. Pixels with different colors that add noise to the image delete color information and replace it with pixels of approximated values. This is shown in the following screenshot:

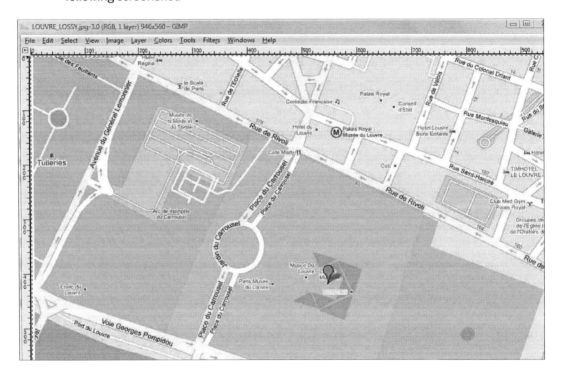

4. It is time to see how .PNG works. This type of image is lossless compression. Follow steps 1 – 3. The difference is that in the **Name** field, type "Louvre_Lossless" and make sure the extension is **PNG image**.

5. The image will be clearer and of a better quality than the previous one. It is shown in the following screenshot:

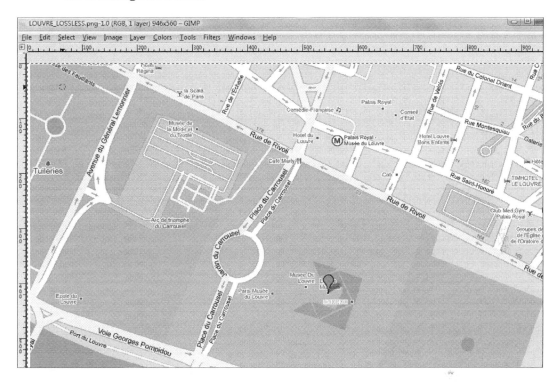

See also

▶ *Chapter 2, Working with 2D and 3D Maps*

▶ *Uploading images to Moodle*

Creating animated graphics

We are going to create animated graphics in order to make our course more appealing. Create different types of animations according to the activity that we want to design. Considering the fact that we are dealing with art and photographs, we can create an animated `gif` about the way a painting was made, or how a place changes in the different seasons and how it looks in different pictures.

Getting ready

Design the animated graphics using the available tools online or using free and open source software. It is very simple, even simpler than its name itself. First of all, bear in mind which pictures you want to insert because neither the software nor the website will add special effects to the pictures to be uploaded.

How to do it...

In this recipe, we will work with a website that creates the animated `gif`. We work with photographs showing different sceneries after selecting the images or photographs to upload. Follow these steps to create the animated graphics:

1. Enter the `http://picasion.com/` website.

2. Click on **Browse** and choose the image that you want to upload.

3. Repeat step 2 multiple times. To add more images, click on **Add one more picture** as many times as required, as shown in the following screenshot:

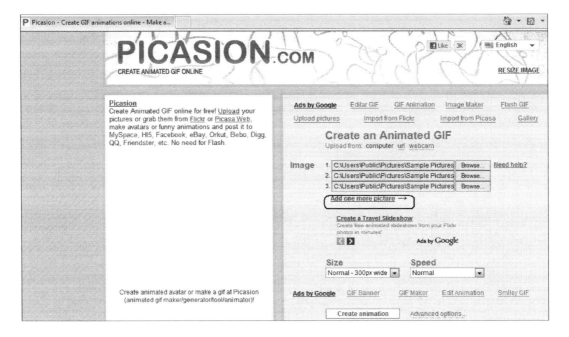

4. Choose the size of the animated graphic. Click on the downwards arrow in the **Size** block.

5. Choose the speed of the animated graphic. Click on the downwards arrow in the **Speed** block.

6. Click on **Create animation**.

7. The animated graphic that you have just created will be displayed. Copy the **HTML code for blog/website** in order to embed it or click on **Save this animation to your computer**, as shown in the following screenshot:

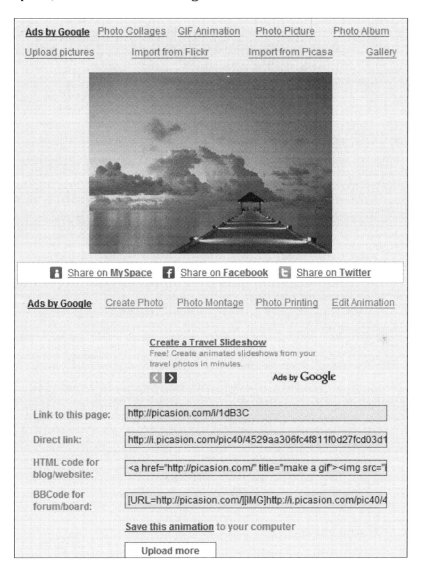

How it works...

We have just created some animated graphics. The following screenshot shows the four frames with images that compose the animated `gif`:

Open the animated `gif` with GIMP that we have already used in the previous recipe. You can see the different animations as layers, as shown in the following screenshot:

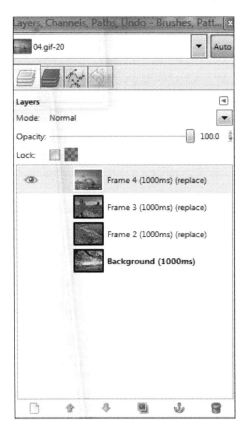

See also

► *Uploading images to Moodle*

Resizing photos to their appropriate size

When working with pictures taken by modern digital cameras, we usually have higher dimensions on the screen. Your Moodle course displays data on the web browser and the web browser usually does not take advantage of the whole screen size. Technology offers devices with different screens; therefore, consider them when dealing with mobile and special devices.

Getting ready

As previously mentioned, there are different screen sizes so the target will be different. Full HD is 1920 x 1080, though it does not fit all the devices, so we will work with 1000 x width and 700 x height as the maximum size of the images.

How to do it...

It is typical that pictures usually have more than 3000 pixels width and 2400 height. We do not want to upload such a huge image to our Moodle course. Thus, we need to resize the photograph to the appropriate height and width values. The larger the image dimensions are, the larger the file sizes are. We will work with GIMP in this recipe too. Therefore, follow these steps in order to resize the image:

1. Click on **File | Open** and browse for the picture to work with.

2. Click on **Save a copy** because you can make a mistake and delete the original image.

3. Write a name for the image and click on **Save** twice.

4. Click on **Image | Scale Image**. Change the aspect ratio. The aspect ratio is the proportion between width and height. You want the same image with fewer pixels.

5. Write 1000 in **Width** within **Image Size**, and **Height** will automatically change to 750. The aspect ratio is calculated automatically.

6. Click on **Scale**, as shown in the following screenshot:

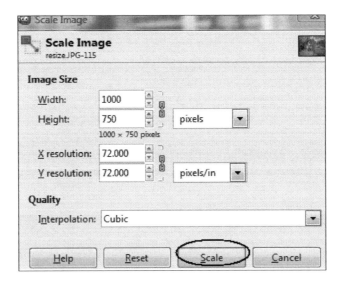

How it works...

We have resized the image, the result of the new resolution 1000 x 750 pixels. If you want a full screen image, check how it looks when you upload it to the Moodle course. You have to save the new image in order to be able to upload it, resized, in our Moodle course. Therefore, click on **File | Save**. Remember that we have saved a copy of the original image previously. The image looks as shown in the following screenshot:

See also

▶ *Selecting between lossy and lossless compression schemes*

▶ *Uploading images to Moodle*

Adding hotspots to photos

In this recipe, we are going to work with photos and add hotspots to them. We use GIMP in order to create them. In *Chapter 3, Working with Different Types of Interactive Charts*, we had created hotspots using a website. In this chapter, we will create them using this free and open source software.

Getting ready

Choose a photo and think of the links that you want to add to it. A good idea related to Art is to choose some famous paintings and add hotspots related to the painter who did them and their biography.

How to do it...

It would be a good idea to resize the image before adding hotspots to it, especially if we are dealing with a photo. Follow these steps in order to add hotspots to the image:

1. Click on **File | Open**. Choose the photo to work with.
2. Click on **Filters | Web | Image map**. The editor block appears and you can add the hotspots.

3. Click on the left-hand margin to choose a shape to map the image. Circle a part of the image to add hotspots. Another pop-up window will appear. Unclick the **Relative link** block. Complete the blocks marked with the links that you want to display, as shown in the following screenshot:

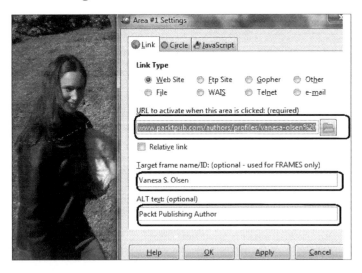

4. Click on **Apply | OK**.

5. The links appear on the right panel.

6. Save the file as .map. Click on **File | Save** and the extension .map will appear automatically. Click on **Save**.

7. You can add as many hotspots to the photo as you want. If so, repeat steps 2 – 4 as many times as hotspots you want to add.

8. When you finish adding hotspots, click on **File | Save**.

9. Click on **View | Source**. A pop-up window displaying the HTML code will appear, as shown in the following screenshot:

How it works...

We have just added a hotspot to the photo. Our photo will not be an ordinary one; when hovering the mouse over the selected area, we will be able to click, and the website that we have selected will appear.

It is time to upload the image to our Moodle course. Therefore, choose the weekly outline section where you want to add the activity and upload the image to the Edit summary section. These are the steps that you have to follow:

1. Click on the **Edit summary** icon in the week that you want to upload the image.
2. If you want to complete the **Section name** block, untick the **Use default section name** box.
3. In the **Summary** block, click on the **Insert/edit image** icon. Click on **Find or upload an image | Upload a file | Browse** and look for the photo that you want to upload.
4. Click on **Upload this file**.
5. Complete the **Image description** block. Click on **Insert**.
6. Click on the **HTML** icon.
7. This is the original HTML code you will see:

    ```
    <p><img alt="hotspots" src="http://localhost/draftfile.php/13/
    user/draft/765594482/Hotspots.JPG" width="1000" height="750" /></
    p>
    ```

8. Insert the following code before `/>`:

    ```
    usemap="#map" border="0"
    ```

9. The code will read as follows:

    ```
    <p><img alt="hotspots" src="http://localhost/draftfile.php/13/
    user/draft/765594482/Hotspots.JPG" width="1000" height="750"
    usemap="#map" border="0"/></p>
    ```

10. Now, insert a new line after the last line and paste the code from GIMP's map source:

    ```
    <map name="map">
    <!-- #$-:Image map file created by GIMP Image Map plug-in -->
    <!-- #$-:GIMP Image Map plug-in by Maurits Rijk -->
    <!-- #$-:Please do not edit lines starting with "#$" -->
    <!-- #$VERSION:2.3 -->
    <!-- #$AUTHOR:Silvina -->
    <area shape="circle" coords="57,241,124" alt="Packt Publishing
    Author" target="Vanesa S. Olsen" href="http://www.packtpub.com/
    authors/profiles/vanesa-olsen%20" />
    </map>
    ```

11. Do not copy the code of the image because you have already uploaded the image into our Moodle course. It was the first step! The final code is:

```
<p><img alt="hotspots" src="http://localhost/draftfile.php/13/
user/draft/803924560/Hotspots.JPG" usemap="#map" border="0"
width="1000" height="750" /></p>
<p>
<map name="map">
<!-- #$-:Image map file created by GIMP Image Map plug-in --> <!--
#$-:GIMP Image Map plug-in by Maurits Rijk --> <!-- #$-:Please do
not edit lines starting with "#$" --> <!-- #$VERSION:2.3 --> <!--
#$AUTHOR:Silvina -->
<area shape="circle" coords="57,241,124" alt="Packt Publishing
Author" target="Vanesa S. Olsen" href="http://www.packtpub.com/
authors/profiles/vanesa-olsen%20" />
</map>
</p>
```

12. Click on **Update**, as shown in the following screenshot:

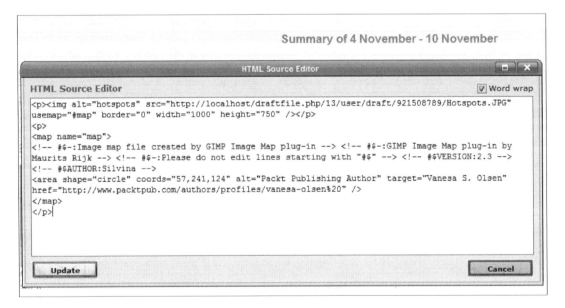

13. Click on **Save changes.**

When hovering the mouse over the image, you will be able to click on the selected image and the website that we have inserted will appear, as shown in the following screenshot:

See also

▶ *Resizing photos to their appropriate size*

Editing color curves

We are going to change the color in our pictures. In this recipe, it would be a good idea to work with the art of your students or with a well-known painting as well, for example to add light or dark to a picture in order to change the perceived time of day.

Getting ready

Choose a photo or a painting for which we want to change its color. We add a bit of our art in order to alter the image. It is a very simple recipe. So, let's see how to do it!

How to do it...

After choosing the photo or painting, run GIMP. Follow these steps in order to edit color curves:

1. Click on **File** | **Open** and browse for the picture that you are going to work with.

2. Click on **Colors** | **Curves**. A pop-up window will appear displaying the curves that you can change.

3. Move the linear histogram to make the image darker or lighter.

4. You can also work with individual channels, that is to say add a value and increase one of the colors shown in the following screenshot. Add green value because the picture shows vegetation. Click on the downwards arrow in **Value** | **Green**, as shown in this screenshot:

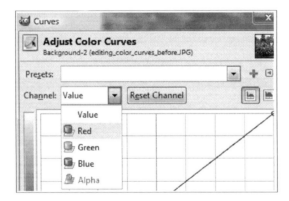

5. When you have finished adjusting color curves, click on **OK**.

6. Save the changes to the photo. Click on **File** | **Save** | **Save**.

How it works...

It is time to see how these curves work on a photo. Therefore, compare the same photo before and after adjusting color curves to it. The following screenshot spots the differences in color. The graph in the right-hand margin shows how we applied the color curve:

See also

▶ *Selecting between lossy and lossless compression schemes*

▶ *Resizing photos to their appropriate size*

▶ *Uploading an image to Moodle*

Adding effects and applying filters

In this recipe, we continue working with GIMP. We apply different effects and filters to the photographs. We can also work with paintings from our own students or famous painters as well. However, in this case, we will deal with photos that we have done in the previous recipes.

Getting ready

First of all, choose the pictures that we want to work with. They can be personal pictures, like the ones that I chose previously, or work with photos from the Internet, but bear in mind the copyright issues. Let's change our photos.

How to do it...

Run GIMP and choose a photo to work in our Moodle course. The sort of effects that we could apply depends on the type of activity that is to be designed. These are the steps to follow:

1. Open the file that you are going to work with. Click on **File | Open** and browse for the photo.

2. Click on **Filters | Artistic | Apply canvas**.

3. There appears the **Apply Canvas** pop-up window.

4. Choose the **Depth** of the canvas; it is circled in the screenshot. You can change the **Depth** from 1 to 50 by clicking on the arrows, as shown inside the square in the following screenshot:

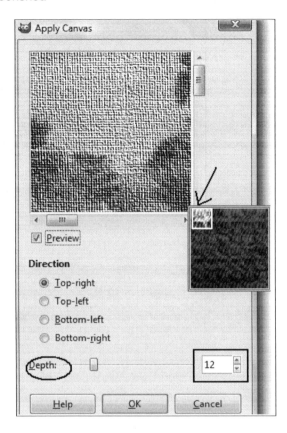

5. **Preview** is ticked in the previous screenshot; therefore, if you click on the four point's arrow, which is not seen in the screenshot but pointed with an arrow, you have the preview of the canvassed photo.

6. When you agree with the changes, click **OK**.

7. Now the photo has the appearance of a canvas. Save the file. Click on **File | Save| Save**.

How it works...

We are going to compare both photos before and after applying the canvas effect. We have worked with a picture of a scenery—the same used in the previous recipe. It would also be a great idea to work with a picture of the face of a person to change that photo into a portrait. So, let's compare the before and after applying the effect. The screenshot shows the photo on the left and the canvas on the right:

There's more

We can also apply other effects on the photos. For example, add the photocopy effect, or change a new picture into an old photo or combine a film strip. Exploring GIMP alternatives to the changes that we can apply to a photo can take a whole chapter of the book, but this is not the aim. The appropriate effect should be selected in relation to the design and/or aim of each activity. Let's explore one more alternative.

Applying an old photo effect to a photo

We are going to work with the old photo effect. In this case, we will work with the picture of two little children. Follow these steps:

1. Click on **File | Open** and browse for the picture that you want to work with.

2. Save the photo with a new name. Click on **File | Save as** and write a new name for the photo.

3. Click on **Filters | Decor | Old Photo**, as shown in the following screenshot:

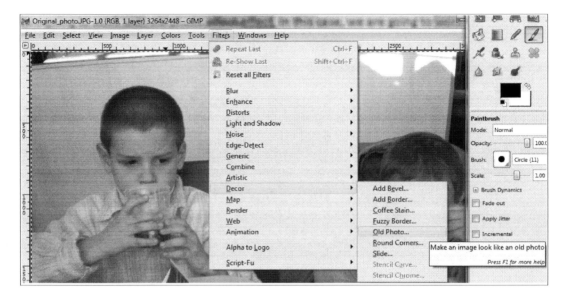

4. There will appear a pop-up window and you may add the changes to the way you want the photo effect, as shown in the following screenshot:

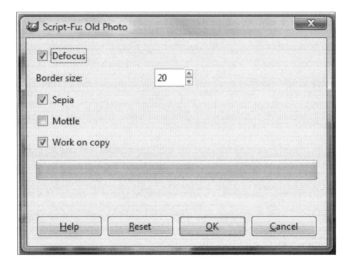

5. Click on **OK**. The following screenshot shows the same photo before on the left and after on the right:

See also

▶ *Selecting between lossy and lossless compression schemes*

▶ *Resizing photos to their appropriate size*

▶ *Uploading images to Moodle*

Uploading images to Moodle

In the previous recipes, we have worked with different types of images, but we have not designed activities with them. The aim of this chapter is to work with images and photographs, so it is time to upload them into our Moodle course.

Getting ready

We are working with art and photographs in this chapter, so we have to design an activity to cope with the previous bitmaps and photographs. Add a map of the Louvre museum to an HTML block in the Moodle course.

We have saved the same image in both formats: . PNG and . JPG. We will insert . PNG in our Moodle course because we have already learnt the difference in quality. When hovering the mouse over the said image, we can click and enter the official website of the Louvre Museum because we are linking the said image with a website.

How to do it...

Enter our Moodle course and follow these steps:

1. Click on the downwards arrow in **Add...** within the block of **Add a block**.

2. Choose **HTML**. When the new block appears, click on the **Configuration** icon.

3. Complete the **Block title**, as shown in the following screenshot:

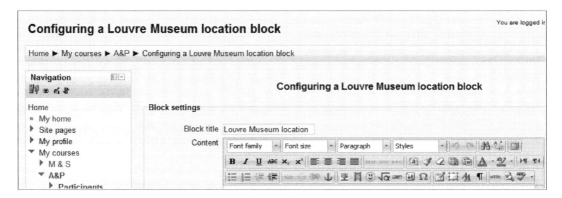

4. In the **Content** block, click on the **Insert/Edit image** icon | **Find or upload an image** | **Upload a file** | **Browse** (you are going to choose the . PNG file).

5. Select the image and click on **Open** | **Upload this file**.

6. Complete the **Description block**.

7. Click on **Appearance**, on the top margin.

8. Click on the downwards arrow in **Alignment** and choose **Middle**.

9. Within **Dimensions**, write **200 x 200 px**.

10. Click on **Insert**.

11. Click on the image and click on the **Insert/Edit link** icon, as shown in the following screenshot:

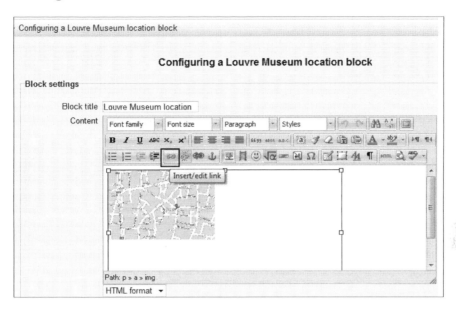

12. Complete the block and make a link to the following website: `http://www.louvre.fr/llv/commun/home.jsp?bmLocale=en`.

13. Click on **Save changes**.

How it works...

We have just uploaded the image of the Louvre Museum that we created to our Moodle course. We did not upload it in the ordinary way; we have made a link to a website using the said image. Therefore, when hovering the mouse over the said image, it will look as shown in the following screenshot:

We can also upload image files in the ordinary way without making links to a website, though it would be sometimes more attractive to our students to do it. Instead of making an ordinary link with words, an icon related to something that they are going to deal with is a good idea to strengthen our Moodle course.

See also

▶ *Selecting between lossy and lossless compression schemes*

▶ *Resizing photos to their appropriate size*

Linking external image files

This is a very simple recipe. We will work with external files in case we need a photo of something specific. Teaching is enhanced when a visual aid is provided to our students, no matter which subject we are teaching. It is sometimes very difficult to have photos of all the things that we want to show them. Thus, we are going to work with Flickr.

Getting ready

Using Flickr to search for photos is an amazing tool due to the fact that we can insert them in our Moodle course in several ways. Copy the link to the file or embed it using the HTML code. Another option is to enable it through our file picker; in this case, we need to switch our role to administrator.

How to do it...

Enter http://www.flickr.com/ and create a free account (we can also upload photos and videos, though this is not the aim). Follow these steps in order to find a photo:

1. Go to the aforementioned website.

2. Click on **Create Your Account**.

3. Complete the pop up that appears with the necessary data. You will have to create a Yahoo! account if you do not happen to have one.

4. Click on **Sign in**.

5. Click on **Sign in** on the right-hand margin.

6. Complete the **Search** block with the type of photo that we need, as shown in the following screenshot:

7. Click on **Search**.

8. Click on **Share this | Grab the link**, as shown in the following screenshot:

9. Copy the link.

10. Another option is to click on **Share this | Grab the HTML/BBCode**.

11. Copy the HTML code to embed in the Moodle course.

How it works...

It is time to upload the art photo in our Moodle course. Choose the weekly outline section where we want to create the activity. Follow these steps in order to insert the images in our Moodle course:

1. Click on **Add an activity | Chat**.

2. Complete the **Name of this chat room** block.

3. In the **Introduction text** block, write what students should do. Click on the **Insert/ edit an image** icon.

4. Paste the link of the photo in the **Image URL** block.

5. Click on **Insert**. Another option is to make a link to the website that displays the photo.

6. Embed another photo. Click on the **HTML** icon.

7. Paste the HTML code of the photo.

8. Click on **Update**.

9. Click on **Save and return to course**.

10. You have created a chat room in which students can share their opinions about these art photos.

8
Working with Vector Graphics

In this chapter, we will cover:

- ▶ Converting vector graphics to bitmap images
- ▶ Rendering parts of a vector drawing
- ▶ Embedding scalable vector graphics
- ▶ Improving vector graphics rendering with anti-aliasing
- ▶ Including vector graphics in Open Office documents
- ▶ Including vector graphics in PDF files
- ▶ Linking to scalable vector graphics
- ▶ Enhancing scalable vector graphics with hyperlinks

Introduction

This chapter explains how to work with different types of vector graphics formats. The recipes use diverse, free, and open source tools to edit, enhance, and convert the different vector graphics files, covering the most common scenarios for multimedia Moodle activities. Vector graphics are one of the most difficult formats to handle in Moodle courses.

The general knowledge topic to be used in the recipes for this chapter is General facts about 2D and 3D Geometry. Different types of activities are to be created using geometrical shapes. You can also create puzzles in order to develop another activity using these types of graphics. We are always eager to insert these graphics in our Moodle activity due to the fact that they strengthen the activities to be performed by our students.

The recipes are organized in such a way that they are linked among themselves. So, it would be a good idea to read the whole chapter in its order without skipping recipes because they add more information as you advance through the recipes. You will also use what you have created in the initial recipes to design the final ones.

It is also very important to read the previous chapter that deals with bitmap images and photographs. There are some aspects considered in that chapter that we are going to cover in this one.

Different types of vector graphics are involved in this chapter due to the fact that they can enhance and create interactive activities. We can not only use them, but also modify them. It is like when you read something and like to share a part of it with your students. Similarly, you can also change the vector graphics in order to use a part of them.

We will cover not just inserting the SVG graphics in Moodle, but also using them in other types of software that can be uploaded to our Moodle courses. You will be working with mainly Inkscape, Open Office, and Adobe Reader. Therefore, it would be a good idea for you to have them installed.

Inkscape is a free and open source vector drawing software to be used in order to perform many recipes. It will allow us to work with many vector assets in several file formats and export them to a format recognized by Moodle. Another possibility is to export the said file format to Hot Potatoes and Quandary 2 used in *Chapter 1, Creating Interactive User eXperiences*.

We can either design the SVG or look for one on the Internet and learn how to do it. Then, we can change it, save as another file extension, and so on. We can also modify it; we may not need to use it per se, but just a part of it. We may insert the SVG in Moodle, or in other types of software such as OpenOffice or PDF, using Adobe Reader.

We are focusing on 2D and 3D Geometry, though the information can be applied to any subject to be taught due to the fact that SVG are needed to enhance our Moodle courses no matter what we are teaching. Images are a great asset to take into account when teaching because students do not read a plain and dull text. They look more appealing when an image is on it.

Converting vector graphics to bitmap images

In this recipe, vector graphics are to be converted into bitmaps. That is to say, we do need to convert them because there is a simple process that we can carry out. It is very easy, but we need to use a free and open source software. Let's get ready!

Getting ready

This transformation process is done with the help of Inkscape. Therefore, if you do not have Inkscape installed, you can download it from the following website: http://inkscape.org/ download/?lang=eng. After downloading it, there are many features that you can learn about and how they work.

How to do it...

After installing Inkscape, search for vector graphics. There is a very interesting website where you can find many kinds of icons: http://www.openclipart.org/browse. Download the SVG clipart and Inkscape will automatically open with the clipart in the middle (if you have previously installed it in your computer). Therefore, follow these steps to start the transformation process:

1. Open your default web browser and enter the website URL.

2. On the top-right margin there appears a **Search** block and type the word 'triangle'.

3. Click on **Search**. Many results showing triangles will appear. Click on one of them.

4. The image will appear bigger. Click on **Download SVG | Open**, as shown in the following screenshot:

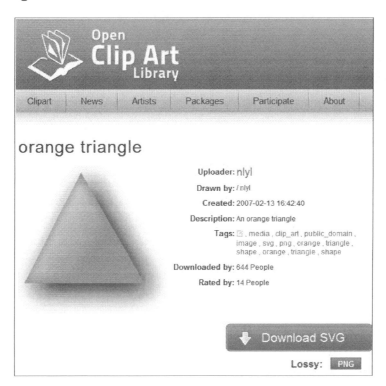

5. Inkscape will open automatically and the clipart will appear, as shown in the following screenshot:

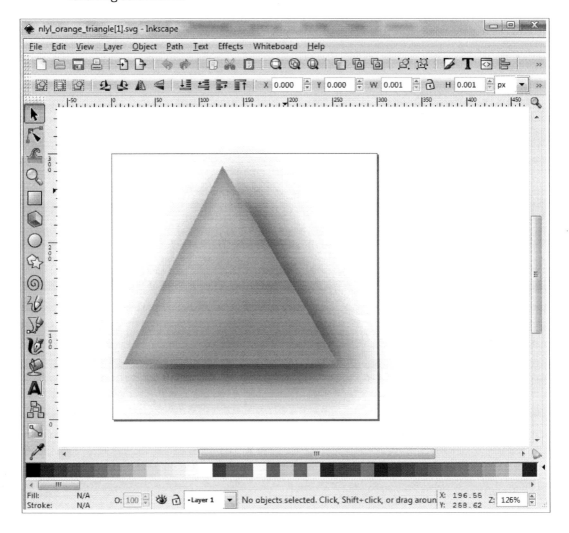

6. Select **File | Save**. Save the file as triangle.svg, for example.

7. Click on **Save**.

How it works...

We have just selected the clipart and saved it in Inkscape as .svg. Now, it is time to transform this .svg into a bitmap (.png file). Therefore, these are the steps to follow in order to carry out the transformation:

1. Click on **File | Export bitmap**, as shown in the following screenshot:

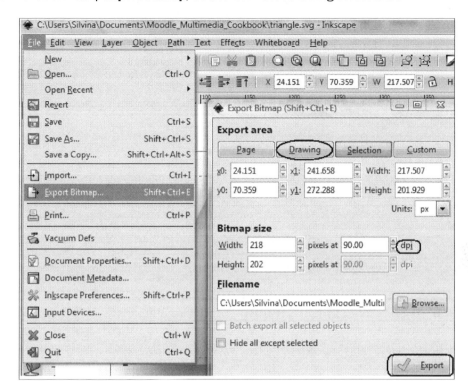

2. **Export area** block will appear showing many export options, as shown in the previous screenshot.

3. Write 30 on the first **dpi** textbox, as shown in the previous screenshot (it says 90).

4. Click on the **Drawing** button, as circled in the previous screenshot.

5. Click on the **Export** button, as shown in the previous screenshot.

6. Inkscape has transformed or exported the drawing in . PNG format.

PNG is an open image format that has lossless compression, as we have already dealt with in *Chapter 7, Working with Bitmap Images and Photographs*. Moodle, Hot Potatoes, and Quandary 2 work very well with these types of files. We have worked with the PNG format due to the fact that the images are small in size.

See also

▶ *Chapter 7, Uploading images to Moodle recipe*

Rendering parts of a vector drawing

In this recipe, we will work with Inkscape (used in the previous recipe). By this time, you must have this software installed on your computer. We will create an SVG using the drawing options in Inkscape that is very simple. After creating the graphic, we will render some of its parts.

Getting ready

In the previous recipe, we worked with a triangle, so let's work with stars, with which we can combine both shapes and create an activity sharing both of them. Imagine that we had the said file, but we want to use only a part of it; it looks as if you have an article in a magazine and you need to take out the advertisement.

How to do it...

Rendering parts of vector graphics means that we use a part of a drawing that we have designed. Therefore, we will not use all the shapes in the file; we will save some of them that we are to select before exporting them. The aim of this recipe is to transform the selection in a bitmap.

Run the Inskape software and follow these steps:

1. Click on **Create stars and polygons (*)** on the left-hand side margin, as shown in the following screenshot:

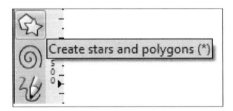

2. Draw several stars of different sizes.

3. Right-click on one of the stars. A pop-up window appears; choose **Fill and Stroke**. Another window on the right-hand margin appears and you can change the color or you can add stripes to the shapes as you click on each of them.

4. When you finish, press the *Shift* key and click on the stars that you want to export as bitmap images.

5. You can move the stars that you want to save onto the left/right-hand margin of the drawing area, as shown in the following screenshot:

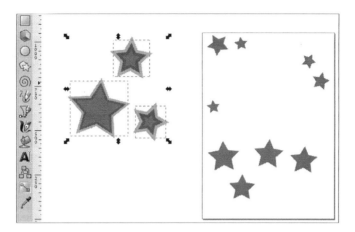

6. Save the file. Click on **File | Save as ...** and write a name for the file.

7. Click on **File | Export Bitmap**. A pop-up window appears. On its ribbon, **Selection** is highlighted. You export the stars that you have selected on the left, as shown in the previous screenshot.

8. Click on **Browse |** and write the name of the file.

9. Click on **Export**.

How it works...

We have just designed the drawing that we want our students to work with. It was a very simple drawing, but we can also do the same process with others that we just want to use a part of. We can check what we have done. We can look for the file in our computer files, and in this case, this is what we have just saved, as shown in the following screenshot:

It is time to Moodle it! We can insert this image in any activity that we want to design in our Moodle course.

See also

▶ *Chapter 7, Uploading images to Moodle*

Embedding scalable vector graphics

This recipe explores different ways of uploading files into our Moodle courses. The steps that we have to follow have to be together, that is to say it is not advisable to do them separately or edit the activity because they might not work.

Getting ready

We are dealing with a pure SVG and it is advisable that we use the Mozilla Firefox web browser because it might not work with other web browsers. You can download it at `http://www.mozilla.com/en-US/products/download.html`. So, let's see how to do this recipe!

How to do it...

We have already used a triangle and stars in the previous recipes, so it is time to change the shape. We can work with a spiral that we can create using Inkscape. Therefore, let's start said software and follow these steps in order to design the SVG to be embedded in our Moodle course:

1. Click on **Create spirals**, as shown in the following screenshot:

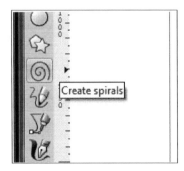

2. Drag-and-drop the spiral shape to the desired size.

3. Click on **File | Save as |** and write a name for the file.

4. Click on **Save**.

How it works...

We have just designed the SVG. Therefore, we need to embed it in our Moodle course. In this recipe, we need to work with some code! Thus, choose the weekly outline section where you want to add the activity. These are the steps that you are going to follow:

1. Click on **Add an activity | Online text**.
2. Complete the **Assignment name** block.
3. Complete the **Description** block, as shown in the following screenshot:

4. Highlight a word or phrase, and click on the **Insert/edit link** icon, as shown circled in the previous screenshot.
5. Click on **Browse** next to the **Link to URL** block.
6. Click on **Upload a file | Browse |** and look for the file that was just created.
7. Click on the file | **Open | Upload this file**.
8. Click on **Insert**. The image will not appear.
9. Click on **HTML Source Editor**. Some code will appear, so edit the code. The following code will appear on the HTML source editor. The only difference will be the location of the file (`"http://localhost/draftfile.php/13/user/draft/168792725/Embed_SVG_Spiral.svg"`):

```
<p><a href="http://localhost/draftfile.php/13/user/
draft/168792725/Embed_SVG_Spiral.svg">Define this.</a></p>
<p>What is it?</p>
<p>Where can you find it?</p>
<p> </p>
<p>
```

10. Add the following code in order to embed the spiral or any SVG file that you want to upload in our Moodle course:

```
<object type="image/svg+xml" data="http://localhost/draftfile.
php/13/user/draft/168792725/Embed_SVG_Spiral.svg">
</object>
</p>
```

11. You must bear in mind that the name of the file previously linked is the same in the code that you insert. Otherwise it won't work!

12. Click on **Update**.

13. Click on **Save and display** to see how it works, as shown in the following screenshot:

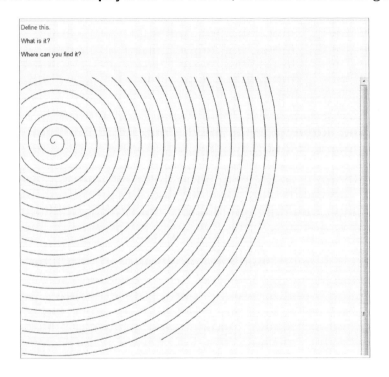

See also

► *Improving vector graphics rendering with anti-aliasing*
► *Chapter 7, Resizing photos to the appropriate size*

Improving vector graphics rendering with anti-aliasing

In this recipe, we will use the previous spiral. Therefore, it means that we also need Inkscape. The aim of this recipe is to export the whole vector graphic as a rendered bitmap with a low resolution. We will take advantage of anti-aliasing.

Getting ready

Anti-aliasing applies intermediate colors in order to eliminate the saw tooth look of pixelated lines. Therefore, we will use Inkscape default anti-aliasing feature to remove the saw tooth effect when rendering the SVG vector graphics to its bitmap representation in a specific resolution.

How to do it...

Start Inkscape software in order to work with an SVG and follow these steps in order to develop the activity:

1. Click on **File | Open**.

2. Open the file created in the previous recipe or draw a spiral of 20 turns. It looks as shown in the following screenshot:

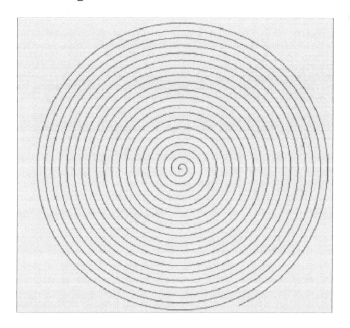

3. Click on **File | Export bitmap**. Complete the pop-up window, as shown in the following screenshot:

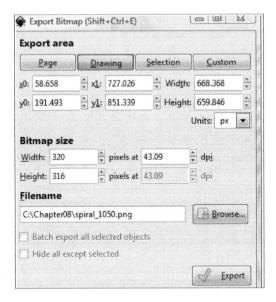

4. Click on **Export**.

How it works...

If we follow the previous steps, we get the rendered bitmap with anti-aliasing applied to it from the source SVG vector graphic. Inkscape applies anti-aliasing by default when we use the export bitmap feature. Therefore, the exported image will look smooth and clear with saw tooth effect reduced, as shown in the following screenshot:

See also

▶ *Chapter 7, Uploading Images to Moodle*

Include vector graphics in Open Office documents

This recipe is very simple and it will be designed using Open Office. We have worked in previous chapters with Spreadsheet and Drawing in Open Office, so it is time to work with Presentation (you could also use Microsoft Office).

Getting ready

It is time to look for an SVG graphic to insert in our presentation. As our baseline topic in this chapter is 2D and 3D Geometry, our SVG is to be with shapes. We can insert the stars designed in a previous recipe. In that case, we can combine the activities in our Moodle course. We can insert the graphic in the weekly outline section to introduce the topic, and we can now use the SVG graphic to design an activity. We can also render the drawing as we did in previous recipes, in that case, we do not want to use all of it.

How to do it...

Click on the Open Office icon to run the software. In this case, choose **Presentation**. Then, these are the steps that you have to follow in order to design the file:

1. When you click on **Presentation**, a pop-up window with the **Presentation Wizard** appears. Click on **Next**.
2. **Select a slide design**, for example, **Numbers on Dark Background** to contrast with shapes, but keeping the Math idea.
3. Click on **Next**.
4. **Select a slide transition**, for example, **Shape Diamond** to keep the shapes idea.

5. Click on **Create**, as shown in the following screenshot:

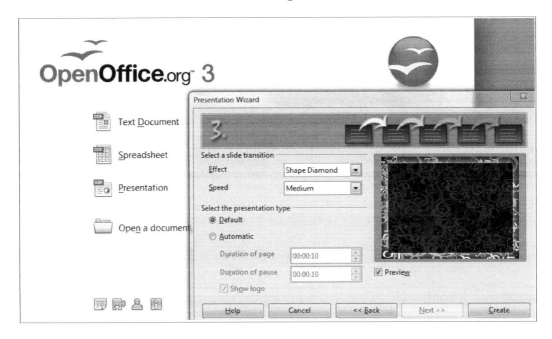

6. It is time to create the presentation. On the right-hand margin, there appears a **Layouts** tab that you may choose in order to design the presentation. Choose the layout with a **Title, Clipart, Text**. When hovering the mouse on them, it says what you can insert, though it is quite clear, as shown in the following screenshot:

7. Double-click on the chosen layout. Then, follow the instructions on the slide to complete it.

8. **Click to add title**, write the title.

9. **Double-click to add graphics**, browse for the SVG to insert, and click on **Open**.

10. **Click to add an outline**. Write the outline. You may write it using bullets.

11. Save the file. Click on **File | Save as ...** | write a name for the file | click on **Save**.

How it works...

After designing the presentation and saving it, we can upload it to our Moodle course. It is the introduction to an activity, therefore, we can add a resource to our course. So, choose the weekly outline section where you want to add the resource and follow these steps:

1. Click on **Add a resource | File**.

2. Complete the **Name** and **Description** blocks.

3. Click on **Add | Upload a file | Browse** and look for the file to be uploaded.

4. Click on **Open | Upload this file**.

5. Within **Options**, click on the downwards arrow in **Display** and choose **Embed**.

6. Click on **Save and return to course**.

7. When students click on the activity, it looks as shown in the following screenshot:

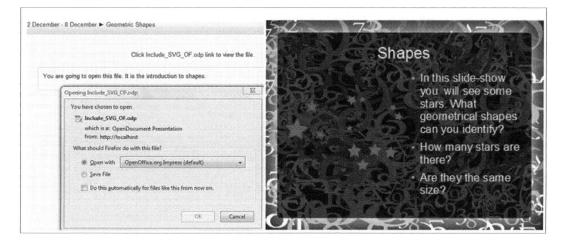

The screenshot on the left shows what students see before opening the file. The screenshot on the right shows the presentation that we have created using Open Office, in which we included SVG.

Include vector graphics in PDF files

This is a very simple recipe. In the previous recipe, we created a file in Open Office in which we included some SVG. So, we can use the same file to work with in order to avoid some steps. Let's get ready!

Getting ready

What we need to have installed is Open Office, which we have already used in previous recipes, and Adobe Reader. We can download the latest software from: `http://get.adobe.com/reader/`.

How to do it...

We open the file in Open Office and we only make a little change to it, in order to export it as PDF. It is very simple, we are just a click away. Start Open Office Presentation and open the file that we created in the previous recipe. Then, follow these steps:

1. Click on **File | Export as PDF**, as shown in the following screenshot:

2. Click on **Export**.
3. Write a name for the file and click on **Save**.

How it works...

We have just saved the file as PDF. It is time to open the file in Adobe Reader. Considering the fact that in the original file there were SVG, it means that when transforming to original file to PDF, we have included SVG in PDF. You can also perform the same procedure using Microsoft Office or any other type of Open Office. In this case, we converted a presentation into a PDF, but we can convert a Text document as well. These are the steps that you have to follow:

1. Run Adobe Reader.

2. Click on **File | Open** and look for the file that you have just saved as PDF.

3. Click on the said file and click on **Open**.

4. The file looks as shown in the following screenshot:

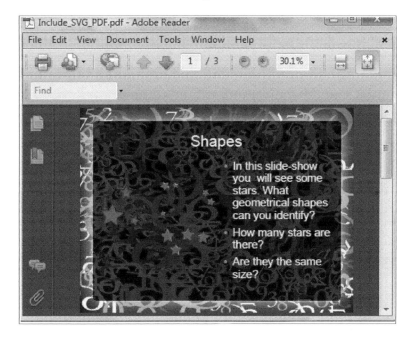

We can upload this file to our Moodle course in the same way that we did in the previous recipe.

Linking to scalable vector graphics

This is a very short and simple recipe. The title tells us what to do. We need to use Inkscape again; we can also use any of the SVG that we have already designed in the previous recipes. We are to upload a PNG image to our Moodle course, and when clicking on the said image, the SVG will appear. We can create many activities using this, especially puzzles.

Getting ready

Our baseline topic in this chapter is 2D and 3D Geometry. Therefore, shapes is the best topic to deal with. Let's choose some 3D shapes that we haven't used yet. When students click on the said shape, another SVG graphic will appear. So, can you think of any interesting activity to design?

How to do it...

Enter your Moodle course and choose the weekly outline section where you want to add the activity. In this case, we will design an online text activity; we'll create a puzzle. Follow these steps:

1. Click on **Add an activity | Online text**.
2. Complete the **Assignment name** block.
3. Complete the **Description** block.
4. Click on the **Insert/edit image** icon | **Upload a file** | **Browse** | look for the file that you want to upload.
5. Click on the file | **Open** | **Upload this file** | **Insert**.
6. Click on the image that you have just uploaded. Click on the **Insert /edit a link** icon.
7. Click on **Browse** next to the **Link URL** block and browse for the SVG file that you want to upload.
8. **Upload a file** | **Browse** | look for the file that you want to upload.
9. Click on the file | **Open** | **Upload this file** | **Insert**.
10. Click on **Save and display**. The activity looks as shown in the following screenshot:

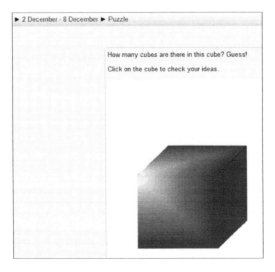

How it works...

When students work on this activity, they are going to be able to click on the image and they are going to open an SVG graphic linked from it. We first uploaded a PNG and the SVG was linked to it. So, this is the way it works, as shown in the following screenshot:

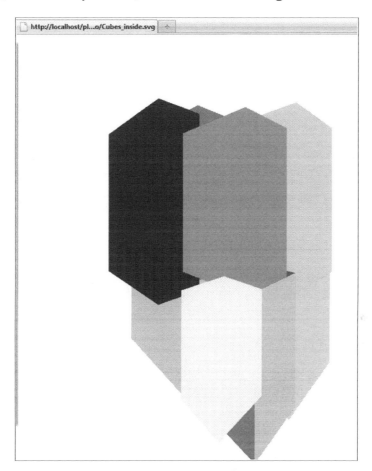

Enhancing scalable vector graphics with hyperlinks

In this recipe, we need to use Inkscape once more. We have become quite familiar with said software. This time, we will create hyperlinks on the SVG graphics. When students click on the image, they will open a website.

Getting ready

Shapes are to be displayed in this activity, as we have done with the previous recipes. Therefore, an interesting idea would be to display a website related to the definition of them or some geometrical information about them.

How to do it...

We need to start Inkscape software in order to design the image and add the hyperlinks. Therefore, follow these steps:

1. Draw some geometrical shapes.
2. Choose one of them and click on it.
3. Right-click on the said shape.
4. There appears a pop-up window. Choose **Create /Link**, as shown circled in the following screenshot:

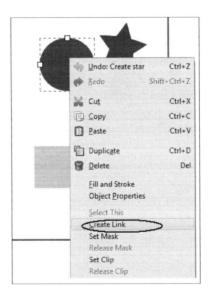

5. Right-click again on the same shape. Click on **Link properties**.
6. Another pop-up window appears. Complete the **Href** with the website that you want to link to, that is to give additional information about the SVG (you may choose any graphic or website related to your subject).
7. Close the pop-up window.
8. Repeat steps 2 – 7 to add hyperlinks to other shapes as required.
9. Save the file. Click on **File | Save as |** write a name for the file.

How it works...

We have just enhanced SVG with hyperlinks using Inkscape software. Therefore, it is time to see how it works. We can upload the graphic to our Moodle course, as we have done in the previous recipes. Another option is to open the file in your web browser. Remember that it is advisable to open SVG files in Mozilla Firefox where these files work properly. When hovering the mouse on the SVG graphic and you click on the graphic, another window will open showing the website of the hyperlink, as shown in the following screenshot:

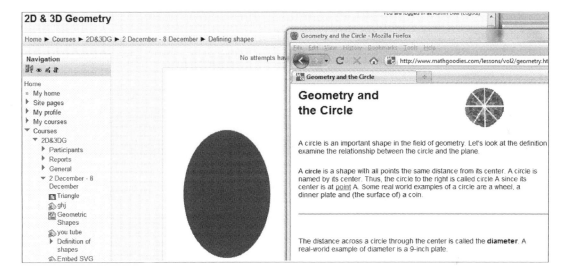

See also

▶ *Embedding scalable vector graphics*

▶ *Linking to scalable vector graphics*

9
Designing and Integrating E-portfolios

In this chapter, we will cover:

- ▶ Enabling a portfolio
- ▶ Preparing a portfolio strategy using a Google Docs portfolio
- ▶ Gathering students' work using a File download portfolio
- ▶ Enabling a Box.net portfolio
- ▶ Using a Box.net portfolio
- ▶ Embedding a Box.net folder in Moodle

Introduction

This chapter explains how to design and integrate e-Portfolios into Moodle courses. We will also learn exciting new techniques to organize the information for our students as well as combine everything learned so far in interacting with e-portfolios.

The recipes are short and precise; beginning with simple portfolios before moving on to more interesting and complex ones. We will take a look at all the portfolios made available until now in Moodle 2.0.

Unfortunately, the three most interesting portfolios available in Moodle 1.9.x—Mahara, Exabis, and MyStuff—are not available at the time of the writing of this book in Moodle 2.x. Therefore, they won't be covered in this chapter.

Another interesting portfolio that is worth paying attention to is Box.net. You need to sign up for an account in order to create an application and get the API key to use it in the Moodle course. An interesting feature of this portfolio is that you can embed a folder in any activity that you design.

An **E-portfolio** (electronic portfolio or digital portfolio) is a collection of electronic evidence gathered and administered by a user on the Web. The evidence should be inputted files, images, and text, among other types of files. Furthermore, E-portfolios in Moodle 2.x enable information to be exported to external systems.

In order to benefit from e-portfolios in Moodle, they must be enabled. Also, as the recipes in this chapter are interrelated, it is best if they read one after another.

When exporting either images or text to a portfolio, we can choose among the ones that we have enabled. Therefore, when dealing with the last recipe, we can select which portfolio to use. After exploring the options that each of them offers, we can decide which portfolio is the best option.

Another characteristic to be considered as an advantage is that portfolios gather files saved on the Web, not on our computer (except for File Download). That is to say, we can change the files anywhere; all we need is an Internet connection, so we just log in and edit the files we need!

We can also share the files and let other students edit them, like in the Wiki activity. We can use Box.net in order to create and embed a folder in our Moodle course in which students can upload files. It only takes some steps, and is a different task that students have to deal with.

To sum up, we could say that e-portfolios are easy to back up, and have a good portability as well as shelf life. Therefore, it would be advisable that we consider them when we design any Moodle course to use them and teach our students to use them too.

The baseline topic of this chapter is History, so we create activities related to that. Besides, the results of the eight previous courses created before is to be considered as well because what we need to export is what our students have written on **Forums**, **Chats**, **Databases**, and other activities that they have carried out.

Enabling a portfolio

The first recipe of this chapter shows how to enable a portfolio in our Moodle course. One of its advantages is that content from our Moodle course can be exported to a virtual and stable external portfolio. So, let's get started!

Getting ready

Before entering the Moodle course that we want to edit, we need to change our role to Manager in order to have access to the Site Administration. When we enable a portfolio we can publish items from our Moodle course to other places to store and organize content.

How to do it...

Enabling a portfolio is a very simple process. After switching roles, we have to follow these steps to enable portfolios in our Moodle course:

1. Click on **Site Administration | Advanced features**, as shown in the following screenshot:

2. Click on **Site Administration | Plugins**.

3. Click on the box next to **Enable portfolios**, as shown in the following screenshot:

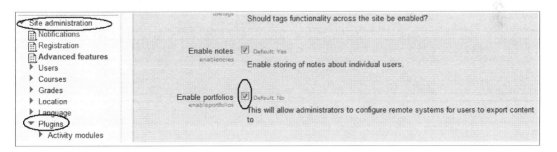

4. Click on **Save changes**.

How it works...

We have just enabled the option portfolio so that it is visible inside the plugins list. There are many portfolios that can be enabled in Moodle 2.0, therefore, follow these steps in order to make them visible:

1. Click on **Site Administration | Plugins | Portfolios | Manage portfolios**, as shown in the following screenshot:

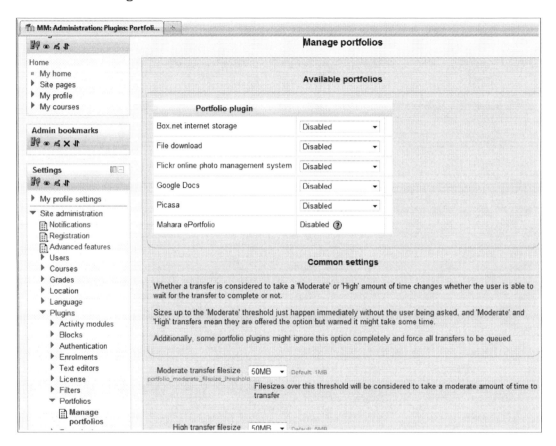

2. Click on the downwards arrow next to **File download** and choose **Enable and visible | Save | Continue**.

3. Repeat step 2 for **Google Docs** and **Picassa**.

4. You have enabled three portfolios, as shown in the following screenshot:

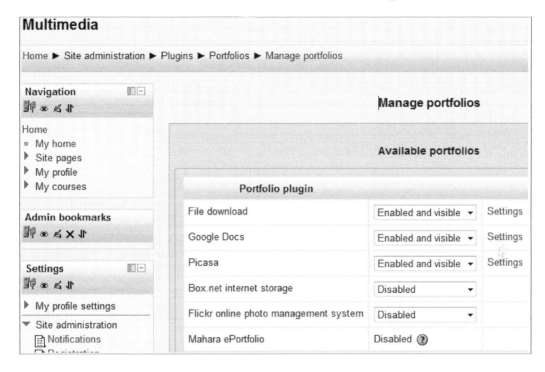

5. Click on **Save changes**.

See also

▶ *Preparing a portfolio strategy using a Google Docs portfolio*

▶ *Gathering students' work using a File download portfolio*

Preparing a portfolio strategy using a Google Docs portfolio

In the previous recipe, we have enabled three portfolios. Therefore, in this recipe, we will work with one of them. We will use the portfolio to save our files in Google Docs, which we have enabled before. We have worked with Google Docs in earlier chapters, so we already have an account in this tool. If you do not have an account, it is necessary to create one.

Getting ready

To see how a Google Docs portfolio works, open your default web browser and go to Google Docs at `https://docs.google.com/`. We enter this website and minimize the screen, when we save a file there, we maximize it in order to compare the files that we have before doing this activity and after we export to the portfolio.

How to do it...

Enter any Moodle course created. Search the results or find a **Forum** activity that we have already created. In this recipe, we enter the course Traveling around the World and Watching the Universe; the course was created during a recipe in *Chapter 2, Working with 2D and 3D Maps*. We will focus on the result of the forum activity Apollo 17. Therefore, these are the steps that we have to follow in order to save a portfolio using Google Docs:

1. Enter the Moodle course. Click on **Apollo 17** forum activity (or any other forum activity that you want to save).

2. Click on the discussion topic that you want to save, in this case **Apollo 17**, as shown in the following screenshot:

3. Click on the downwards arrow to select the way you want to see the forum answers, as shown in the following screenshot:

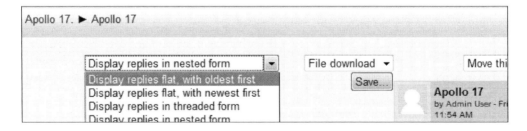

4. Next to the aforementioned block (the one that you choose how the information is to be displayed), there appears the **Save** button. Click on the downwards arrow and choose **Google Docs**, as shown in the following screenshot:

5. Click on **Save**. The following message appears, as shown in the following screenshot:

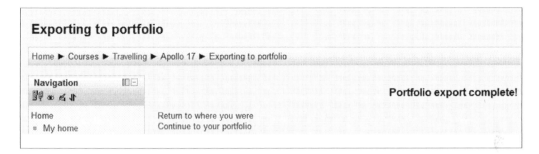

6. You can choose to **Return to where you were** or **Continue to your portfolio**. Thus, click on the place where you want to go.

How it works...

At the beginning of the recipe, we entered the Google Docs account and saw our files in the said website. Thus, when we click on **Continue to your portfolio**, as shown in the previous screenshot, we can see that the discussion in the forum was successfully saved in our Google Docs account, as shown in the following screenshot:

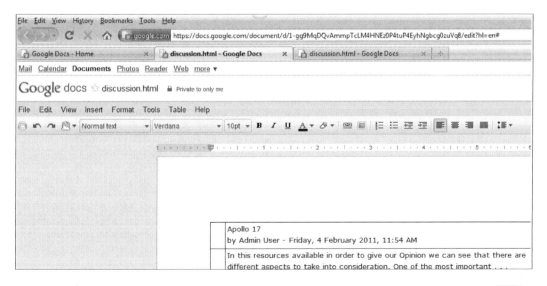

Gathering students' work using a File download portfolio

Gathering our students' work is one of the characteristics of portfolios. Therefore, in this recipe we deal with File download. Through this portfolio, we can save the homework done in a simple way. The first step that we should bear in mind is to create a folder in which we save all the files, in order to organize ourselves.

Getting ready

We enter a course where we need to grade a student's activity. In this case, we save the result of a Chat activity that was created in a History course. Students discuss Medieval England after dealing with different resources.

How to do it...

We have to enter the Chat activity in order to save our students' conversations. We can also carry out similar steps if we want to save the opinions of our students through a Forum activity. These are the steps that we have to follow:

1. Enter the **Chat** activity that was done by the students.

2. Click on **View past chat sessions**, as shown in the following screenshot:

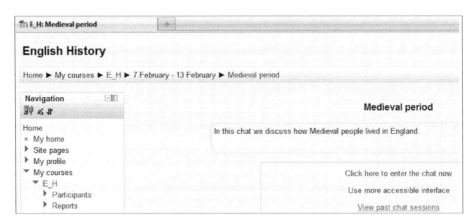

3. Click on **List all sessions** and select the session that you want to save.

4. Click on **Export to portfolio**, next to the **File download** option, as shown in the following screenshot:

5. A pop-up window appears displaying the information about which software the file will be opened in. Click on **OK**, as shown in the following screenshot:

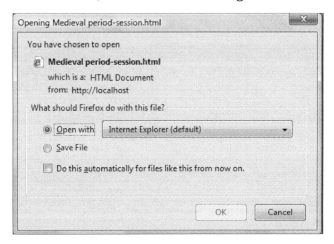

6. The file appears in our default web browser. Click on **Return to where you were** in the Moodle course and go back to the course.

How it works...

The file was opened with our default web browser, and we can save it so as not to lose it. Therefore, follow these steps:

1. Click on **Page | Save as** giving a name for the file, as shown in the following screenshot:

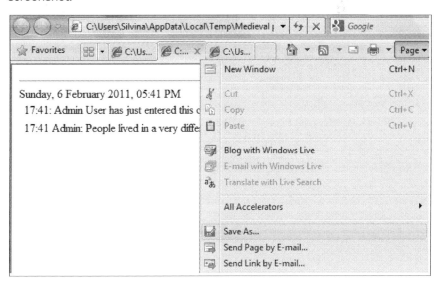

2. Click on **Save**.

We have already exported the chat session of our students and saved it in our computer. On the left-side of the screenshot, there appears the chat session of our students.

Enabling a Box.net portfolio

Box.net is a portfolio that can also be enabled in our Moodle course. It is not as simple as the other portfolios that we have enabled; we just need one more step to enjoy its advantages. We need to enter `http://www.box.net/` and sign up to create an account.

Bear in mind that during this recipe we must switch our roles to Managers in order to be able to have access to enable this portfolio.

Getting ready

There are two Box.net plans available. One of them is free of charge that happens to be personal and the business one is paid. We choose the personal one that is free. After that, we set up our account after completing some information.

How to do it...

It is time to get the Box.net API key to enable the portfolio. API stands for Application Programming Interface. Moodle incorporates third-party API so that portfolio developers can develop more efficient plugins in order to integrate portfolios in Moodle 2.x.

In order to get the Box.net API key, enter the following website: `http://www.box.net/developers/services` and create a new application. These are the steps to follow:

1. Click on **Create new Application**.
2. Read the terms and conditions and click on **Accept**.

3. Complete the **General information** required, as shown in the following screenshot:

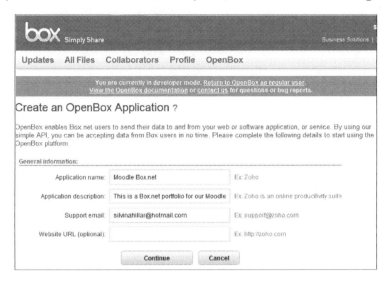

4. Complete the **website URL**, which is optional with the URL provided by our Moodle course. Therefore, leave that block aside and minimize this window for a moment.

5. Open your Moodle course and switch role to Administrator.

6. Click on **Site Administration | Plugins | Portfolios | Manage portfolios**.

7. Click on the downwards arrow next to **Box.net internet storage** and select **Enabled and visible**.

8. Copy the URL that appears, as shown in the following screenshot:

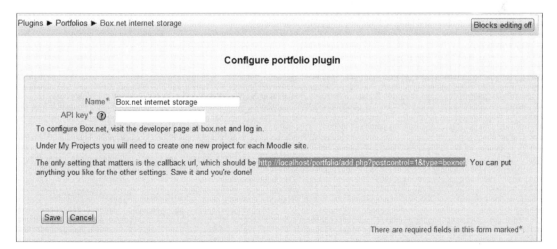

9. Minimize the screen (do not close it).

10. Maximize the Box.net website (that was minimized), and paste the URL you have just copied in the block that was left aside in step 4. Click on **Continue**.

11. Another screenshot appears with the **API key** that you need to paste in the Moodle course, as shown in the following screenshot:

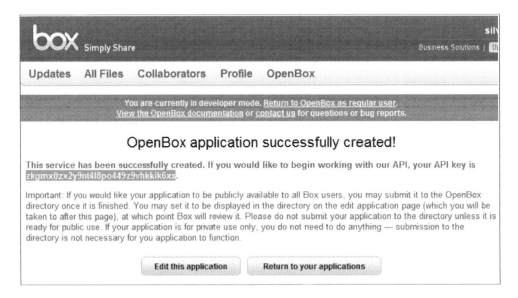

12. Copy the **API key**, and minimize this web browser.

13. Go back to the Moodle course and paste the **API Key** in the blank block.

14. Click on **Save | Continue | Save changes**. The portfolio has been successfully enabled.

How it works...

On the left-hand margin of our Moodle course under **Site administration heading | Plugins | Portfolios** appears **Box.net internet storage** (now visible). Therefore, it means that we enabled the said portfolio, as shown in the following screenshot:

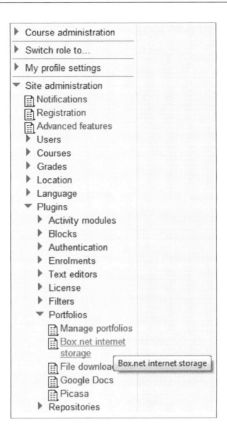

See also

- ▶ *Using a Box.net portfolio*
- ▶ *Embedding a Box.net folder in Moodle*

Using a Box.net portfolio

In this recipe, we work with Box.net, the portfolio that we have just enabled in the previous recipe. Therefore, as we have already worked in previous recipes with other portfolios, we will focus on this one in this task.

Getting ready

We can open our default web browser and log in to our account in order to see how the export to this portfolio works. Therefore, enter `http://www.box.net/` and log in to your account, the one that we have created before.

How to do it...

First of all, we need to select what files we want to export to Box.net. Therefore, enter a Moodle course and choose a **Forum** activity that students have worked in. These are the steps to follow:

1. Enter any Moodle course and click on a **Forum** activity.
2. Click on the name of the discussion topic.
3. Click on the downwards arrow and select **Box.net internet storage**, as shown in the following screenshot:

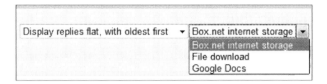

4. Click on **Save**.
5. Tick the **Share this file?** and **Share this new folder?** blocks (shown in the screenshot after step 6).
6. Click on the downwards arrow and choose **Moodle portfolios (shared)**, as shown in the following screenshot:

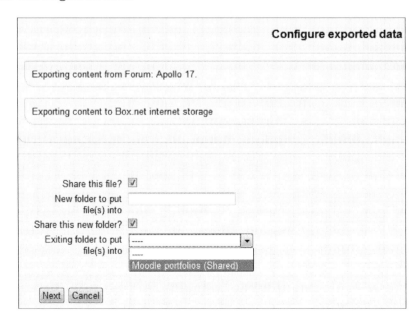

7. Click on **Next**.

8. The following information appears, as shown in the following screenshot:

9. Click on **Continue**.
10. The portfolio export is complete. You can **Return to where you where** or **Continue to your portfolio**.

How it works...

We have just successfully exported our portfolio, but we have not seen it. Thus, if we click on **Continue to your portfolio**, we can see that we have just saved our file in Box.net. Therefore, the Forum discussion appears, as shown in the following screenshot:

Note that next to updates, **1NEW** appears. It means that there is the file that we have just exported from our Moodle course. Click on the file to see what students have written in said Forum activity.

See also

▶ *Enabling a Box.net portfolio*

▶ *Embedding a Box.net folder in Moodle*

Embedding a Box.net folder in Moodle

This is a very interesting way to use a portfolio. It is sometimes advisable to use portfolios in different ways so that we do not get used to the same process. Besides, designing activities that are not alike enhances the course. We will embed a Box.net folder in our Moodle course.

Getting ready

We have to create an activity in this recipe because we need to embed a folder in it. The purpose is that students should upload a file in this folder. Its advantage is that we are using the portfolio directly from our Moodle course.

How to do it...

Before embedding a Box.net folder in our Moodle course, we need to create a folder to embed. Apart from that, we need to choose the characteristics of the said folder. Log in to your Box.net account and follow these steps in order to create a folder:

1. Click on **Files** on the upper ribbon.

2. Click on the downwards arrow in **New** and choose **Folder**, as shown in the following screenshot:

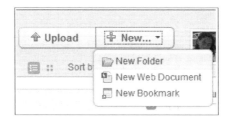

3. Complete the **Folder Name** block.

4. Click on the ring button **Invite people to upload or download files**.

5. Click on the downwards arrow in **Access Type** and choose **Editor**.

6. Click **Okay**.

7. The folder has been created, as shown in the following screenshot:

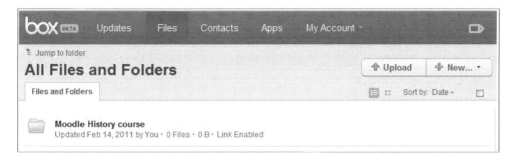

8. Click on the folder you have just created, in this case **Moodle History course**, as shown in the previous screenshot.

9. Click on the downwards arrow in the **Folder Options** block, as shown in the following screenshot:

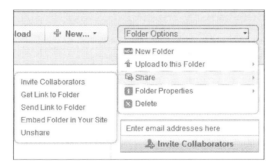

10. Click on **Share | Embed folder in your site** (if you do not want to embed the folder you can click on **Get Link to Folder** and copy the URL. You can make a link in the Moodle course). A pop-up window appears, as shown in the following screenshot:

11. Copy the HTML code and click on **Close**.

How it works...

We have just copied the HTML code that we need to paste in our Moodle course in order to embed the Box.net folder. Therefore, we now need to create an activity. Follow these steps:

1. Click on **Add an activity | Offline activity** within **Assignments**.

2. Complete the **Assignment name** and **Description** blocks.

3. Click on the **Edit HTML source** icon and paste the HTML code.

4. Click on **Update**.

5. Click on **Save and display**. The activity looks as shown in the following screenshot:

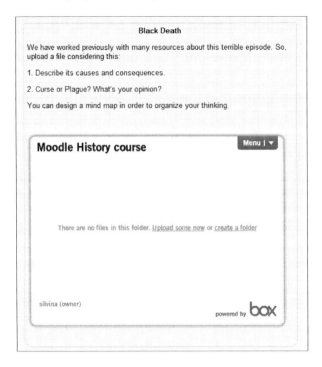

See also

▶ *Enabling a Box.net folder in Moodle*

▶ *Using a Box.net portfolio*

Index

Thank you for buying
Moodle 2.0 Multimedia Cookbook

About Packt Publishing

Packt, pronounced 'packed', published its first book "*Mastering phpMyAdmin for Effective MySQL Management*" in April 2004 and subsequently continued to specialize in publishing highly focused books on specific technologies and solutions.

Our books and publications share the experiences of your fellow IT professionals in adapting and customizing today's systems, applications, and frameworks. Our solution based books give you the knowledge and power to customize the software and technologies you're using to get the job done. Packt books are more specific and less general than the IT books you have seen in the past. Our unique business model allows us to bring you more focused information, giving you more of what you need to know, and less of what you don't.

Packt is a modern, yet unique publishing company, which focuses on producing quality, cutting-edge books for communities of developers, administrators, and newbies alike. For more information, please visit our website: www.packtpub.com.

About Packt Open Source

In 2010, Packt launched two new brands, Packt Open Source and Packt Enterprise, in order to continue its focus on specialization. This book is part of the Packt Open Source brand, home to books published on software built around Open Source licences, and offering information to anybody from advanced developers to budding web designers. The Open Source brand also runs Packt's Open Source Royalty Scheme, by which Packt gives a royalty to each Open Source project about whose software a book is sold.

Writing for Packt

We welcome all inquiries from people who are interested in authoring. Book proposals should be sent to author@packtpub.com. If your book idea is still at an early stage and you would like to discuss it first before writing a formal book proposal, contact us; one of our commissioning editors will get in touch with you.

We're not just looking for published authors; if you have strong technical skills but no writing experience, our experienced editors can help you develop a writing career, or simply get some additional reward for your expertise.

Moodle 1.9 for Second Language Teaching

ISBN: 978-1-847196-24-8   Paperback: 524 pages

Build robust and reliable persistence solutions for your enterprise Java application

1. A recipe book for creating language activities using Moodle 1.9

2. Get the most out of Moodle 1.9's features to create enjoyable, useful language learning activities

3. Create an online language learning centre that includes reading, writing, speaking, listening, vocabulary, and grammar activities

Moodle 1.9 E-Learning Course Development

ISBN: 978-1-847193-53-7   Paperback: 384 pages

A complete guide to successful learning using Moodle

1. Updated for Moodle version 1.9

2. Straightforward coverage of installing and using the Moodle system

3. Working with Moodle features in all learning environments

4. A unique course-based approach focuses your attention on designing well-structured, interactive, and successful courses

Please check **www.PacktPub.com** for information on our titles